I hope that the Nobel Peace Prize awarded me will send this message to the world: that the other 50 percent of the world—the women of the world—that their skills, talents and intelligence should be utilized. And I think this message is a resounding agreement to all of our advocacies over the years. That truly women have a place, truly women have a face and truly the world has not been functioning well without the input, in every sphere, of women.

From an interview of Leymah Gbowee
Liberian lawyer, Nobel Peace Prize winner 2011

WOMEN IN LAW

Virginia Lalli

AuthorHouse™ LLC
1663 Liberty Drive
Bloomington, IN 47403
www.authorhouse.com
Phone: 1-800-839-8640

Published by AuthorHouse 02/25/2014

ISBN: 978-1-4918-6454-8 (sc)
ISBN: 978-1-4918-6452-4 (hc)
ISBN: 978-1-4918-6353-4 (e)

Library of Congress Control Number: 2014903060

Any people depicted in stock imagery provided by Thinkstock are models,
and such images are being used for illustrative purposes only.
Certain stock imagery © Thinkstock.

This book is printed on acid-free paper.

Because of the dynamic nature of the Internet, any web addresses or links contained in
this book may have changed since publication and may no longer be valid. The views
expressed in this work are solely those of the author and do not necessarily reflect the
views of the publisher, and the publisher hereby disclaims any responsibility for them.

To women,
those who have been my life models
and to their generating force.

INTRODUCTION

In this book, I have sought to collect the stories of women who have achieved significant accomplishments in the field of law and thus contributed to its evolution.

I came across some of these stories while studying and researching human rights; others, from reading news and current affairs; others yet, I "encountered" during my career.

The oldest in time is the Biblical judge Debora: her wisdom and faith in justice led her to become a triumphant chieftain. We then have Antigone: in Sophocles' tragedy, she defied a royal edict because it conflicted with her sense of respect for individuals and with divine law. Next is Eleanor of Arborea, a lawmaker who anticipated the concept of citizen equality and an early form of women's rights by several centuries.

Probably few readers are aware that the Nobel Peace Prize was created thanks to a woman: Bertha Von Suttner, who understood the value it could have in particularly belligerent historical times. Her veiled figure on the Austrian 2 Euro coins may, however, be familiar to many.

I will show that women have played a decisive role in drafting laws and treaties. The 1948 Declaration of Human Rights originated from Eleanor Roosevelt's tenacity, charisma and far-sightedness. The 1989 International Convention on the Rights of the Child was brought about by the vision and generosity of the intrepid Eglantyne Jebb. It is thanks to Jody Williams' courageous initiative that the first Mine Ban Treaty was drafted in 1997.

The book also traces the lives of Italy's first female lawyer—Lidia Pöet—and first practicing female barrister, Lina Furlan. It discusses the suffragettes and their battles to achieve women's rights to vote, to actively participate in political life and to education.

As for our contemporaries, I will explore the lives of Hillary Clinton, Shirin Ebadi and Michelle Obama, all women who focused their practice of the legal profession to support the defense of children, women and the disadvantaged, and ensure equal opportunities for all.

Finally, the book will examine the claim to equal labor rights advanced by Ford's female workers, during their 1968 Dagenham strike, and the story of factory worker Crystal Lee Sutton. We will see that femininity and Law, passion and the Code have characterized the endeavors of "women in law".

I also wish to commemorate all the less famous "women in law" whom I have had the good fortune to meet personally. The women of the *Movimento per la Vita* who, competently and caringly, defend conceived children. The women of the End Child Prostitution, Pornography and Trafficking Association (ECPAT) who fight sexual tourism and child trafficking. The women of the *Associazione Italiana Amici di Raoul Follereau* (AIFO) who promote the culture of human rights in schools. The volunteers of the *Associazione 99 gatti dell'Aquila* and of other movements who care for abandoned animals.

Finally, I turn my thoughts to the future "women in law" who are only just starting out; may they preserve the memory of those who tread before them . . .

Virginia Lalli

CONTENTS

CHAPTER 1

DEBORA

Female judge, prophet and warrior

When Moses led the Israelites out of Egypt, they crossed a vast desert before coming to the shores of the Jordan River—the only great river in Palestine—which was also a border. Although their leader only managed to see it from afar, the Israelites had finally reached the Promised Land. According to God's promise to Abraham, this was a wonderful land "of milk and honey", with mountains, hills, valleys, plains, forests and springs in abundance. Its name was Canaan and its dwellers were the Cananaeans, who had built small fortified towns, cultivated the fertile land and worshipped their gods Baal and Astarte. The Israelites' arrival completely overwhelmed their lives.

The year is *circa* 1150 BCE. After Moses' death, Joshua became the new leader. Seeing the Cananaeans worship Baal and other gods, the Israelites wondered whether they too should worship other divinities to obtain a good harvest; thus, they began to be unfaithful to their God.

When Joshua died, the military and political unity of the Jewish people fell apart, and the manifold different patriarchal groups broke away from one another.

The Cananaeans began to attack them, seeking to reduce them into slavery or to drive them away. The Cananaean king Jabin was the ruler of Hasor; Sisara was the leader of his army. The children of Israel cried out to their Lord in despair, because Jabin had "nine hundred chariots fitted with iron, and had been oppressing them with violence for twenty years" (Judges 4, 1-3). The Israelites' lives were in danger:

travel was unsafe, anarchy ruled and all could do as they pleased; the people began to worship idols. In other words, they were in desperate need of a leader—a Judge, a figure who enjoyed great authority over neighboring peoples too:

"All village life had ceased, it had ceased in Israel, until I, Deborah, arose, arose as mother in Israel. Foreign gods were worshipped and, at that time, war was nigh" (Judges 5, 7-8).

The roles of prophet, judge and warrior were all combined in one woman.

The Book of Judges introduces Deborah as the wife of Lappidot (Judges 4, 4), but her husband plays no part in the narration; we know nothing of him other than his name. He does not have any particular role to fulfill, while she, on the other hand, was already well-known by the time she took command of the government and became the "mother of Israel" (Judges 5, 7) and savior of her land thanks to her courageous commitment to defending her people.

Deborah enjoyed special renown as a prophet and a sage who adjudicated and resolved disputes among the Israelites. She was the knowledge that establishes justice, an illuminated woman who had a particularly close relationship with the God of Israel: she was the enlightened prophet, the mouth of God for his people. The Israelites consulted her in multitudes, climbing the Ephraim mountain between Rama and Betel; here, Debora would receive them in the open air, seated under a palm tree that bore her name (in the ancient East, the palm tree was sacred and symbolized the glory of God—the walls and the shutters of the Holiest of the Holy in Solomon's Temple were decorated with palm trees: 1 Kings 6, 29-35).

"[The] Israelites went up to her to have their disputes decided . . ." (Judges 4, 4-5). For the first time after Moses' death, the role of prophet was fulfilled by a woman, Debora. It is she who acted as the intermediary between God and the people.

"Debora does not fear facing those who are powerful, and is the only woman who receives the title of "judge". The Word of God makes her free to listen to the problems and lamentations of those who turn to her seeking justice, advice and spiritual guidance, and she shows the

Israelites the path of faithfulness to God. Debora is close to people's lives; her prophetic vocation is expressed through a special talent for listening and spiritual understanding, which is surprisingly in touch with daily life. Debora would calmly sit under her palm tree and listen to those who sought her in this natural setting, in direct contact with the earth, God's gift to his people. With Debora, we are not on sacred ground. Rather, God's glory reveals itself in his creation, under the palm tree where the prophet-judge listens to the people's problems. Debora draws people to her with her wisdom. She is a woman who resolves issues and seeks peace. What is the good of sowing seeds, working and cultivating the land, if the enemy then seizes the harvest? What is the use of being free from Egypt, if one is a slave in one's own land? Debora listens to complaints, and gives advice and encouragement. The shade of the palm tree under which she sits evokes the Divine Presence, recalling the shade cast by the cloud that guided Israel through the desert (see Es 13, 22; 19, 16). God does not abandon his People. He always finds men and women who can hear the Word and lead on the path to freedom. Under Debora's palm tree, the prophecy expresses itself in a female declination.[1]

Debora thus revealed the glory of God, a glory that manifested itself as justice and freedom from oppression, in the complex turns of history. Debora took the initiative to summon the Israelite general Barak (whose name means "thunderbolt") and to show him the divine oracle, which ordered him to enlist ten thousand men and face the enemy's army: "The Lord God of Israel gives you this command: go, take with you ten thousand men of Naphtali and Zebulun and lead them up to Mount Tabor. I will lead Sisara, the commander of Jabin's army, with his chariots and troops to the Kishon River and give him into your hands." General Barak hesitated. He feared defeat and told Debora: "[i]f you go with me, I will go; but if you don't go with me, I will not go" (Judges 4, 8), so that he could consult God through the prophet during the battle. Indeed, Debora was the one to impart courage and indicate the correct strategies to Barak's improvised army, against the enemy king Sisara, his troops and his nine hundred war chariots. Debora agrees to accompany Barak to war, but announced that the honor of victory will belong to a woman. "Certainly I will go with you [. . .] But because of the course you are

---

[1]   Elena Bosetti, *Donne delle Bibbia*, Cittadella Editrice, Assisi, 2009, p. 39.

taking, the honor will not be yours, for the Lord will deliver Sisara into the hands of a woman" (Judges 4, 9).

It is Debora who decided the day upon which the battle was to take place (Judges 4, 14). The army follows, and at the right moment, she told Barak: "Go! This is the day the Lord has given Sisara into your hands. Has not the Lord gone ahead of you?" Debora was the leader of the battle; God, not Barak, was victorious.

Debora was at Barak's side on the Tabor mountain, certain of God's intervention. Once Sisara learnt that Barak had gone up to the Tabor, he brought his nine hundred chariots and the entire army from Haroset-goim to the Kishon River. Debora turned to Barak: "Rise, this is the day that the Lord will deliver Sisara into your hands, the Lord himself will be your guide". Barak descended from the Tabor with his ten thousand soldiers. The Lord "routed Sisara and all his chariots and army by the sword".

Debora called for rain, and Israel won: the Cananaeans' chariots were mired down in the Kishon swamps. On the shores of the Kishon River, another miracle happened: the River, just like the Red Sea, flooded the powerful army, and the God of Israel reversed the outcome once again. After a long fight, Barak followed the chariots and the enemy was defeated" (Judges 4, 1-16).

Sisara leapt down from his horse and fled on foot, but he died by the hand of a woman, Jael.

Contrary to what one may guess, the woman to whom the victory was attributed and into whose hands Sisara was delivered was not Debora. Indeed, the prophet had foretold: "Sisara fled on foot to the tent of Jael, the wife of a relative of Moses. Jael went out to meet Sisara and said to him 'Come, my lord, come right in. Don't be afraid.' So he entered her tent, where she offered him some water. After making him believe that she was guarding the tent, Jael quietly returned to the tent and killed him with a hammer. When Barak came by in pursuit of Sisara, she went out to meet him saying 'Come, I will show you the man you seek.' Barak went in and saw Sisara, dead" (Judges 4, 17-22).

"The region had peace for forty years", according to the Book of Judges (5, 31). Israel regained its unitary strength, which had not been possible for years because all "village life" had ceased and each tribe had fended for itself, without any inter-tribal sense of fraternity or solidarity whatsoever. Israel had needed a "mother", had needed Debora, for its regeneration. "It is she who recalls that life is struggle and fight, that one cannot remain silent before evil and injustice, that the fraternal conscience and sense of personal responsibility must be rekindled. Debora taught the people how to listen to the Word and to re-establish justice, to strive for peace under the palm tree, to remain faithful to God and to continue to praise the Lord, God of Israel"[2]

The heroine remains Debora, enterprising, wise, brave, loyal. After the victory, she raised her most famous hymn to Yahweh and keenly invited all to bless the Lord who frees his people from enemies.

---

[2]   *Ibidem*, p. 41.

CHAPTER 2

ANTIGONE

The conflict between man-made laws and divine laws

Creon: "You differ from all these Thebans in that view".
Antigone: "They too share it; but they curb their tongues for you."

Antigone: "I know that I please where I am most bound to please."

(from Sophocles' *Antigone*)

The protagonist of Sophocles' tragedy is Antigone, a woman who challenged the laws of the *polis*: in particular, King Creon's edict forbidding her brother's burial, contrary to religious prescriptions. Burial rites were then an extremely significant form of recognition and respect for the deceased, and absolutely sacrosanct for Antigone. Indeed, she profoundly opposed the injustice and flouted the Sovereign's orders.

The tragedy thus focuses on a moral and religious dilemma. King Creon denied "the honor of burial" to Polyneices' body because he had betrayed his city, Thebes, by waging war against it: the King ordered his body to be left unburied, so that "carrion dogs, or birds" would devour it. The funeral rites were to be respected, instead, for Polyneices' brother Eteocles, who died defending Thebes.

Antigone confided in her sister Ismene her plan to bury their brother Polyneices, and asked her to join in fulfilling their fraternal duty. Antigone saw this duty as natural, and as such, unquestionable.

"To the first objections raised by timid Ismene, Antigone replies that failing to bury Polyneices is tantamount to "betraying" him. Then, when Ismene tries to persuade her that women cannot fight against men, and that she will pray to their dead brother to forgive them, Antigone stops trying to convince her sister, and no longer considers her as being of the same blood: she disowns her once and for all"[3].

In her struggle to defend the divine laws, Antigone cannot count on anyone but herself. She will have to perform the funeral rites for Polyneices alone.

Thus, the contrast between Antigone's heroic humanity and Ismene's "common" humanity emerges. The play's next scene features the old Thebans saluting the dawning sun and the liberation of their city—their victory against the enemy. Creon solemnly proclaims his edict and makes a display of his skill in ruling. He orders Polyneices' unburied body to be guarded by soldiers, but Antigone is watching, concealed. Taking advantage of the guards' distraction, she quickly performs the funeral rites for her brother. One of the guards who were supposed to watch the body reports to Creon that the edict has been violated: the body was covered with earth for burial, and the funeral rites necessary for his peace in Hades had been performed. A guard leads Antigone, captured, before King Creon. The ensuing dialogue between her and the king constitute the core of the tragedy. Antigone exalts divine law: her words strike the king "in his sense of arbitrary authority, in his pride, in his greed for power"[4].

To Creon's long speech, Antigone simply replies "Will you do more than take and slay me?" To his response that her death will suffice, she persists: "Why then do you delay? In your discourse there is nothing that pleases me,—never may there be!—and so my words can only be unpleasing to you. And as for glory—how could I have won nobler glory than by giving burial to my own brother?"

"Antigone's position is absolute: on one hand, there is good, on the other there is evil. There is no space at all for accommodation, negotiation, or discussion"[5].

---

[3]   G. Perrotta, *Disegno storico della letteratura greca*, Principato Editore, Milan, 1964, p. 132.

[4]   *Ibid.*

[5]   *Ibid.*

7

However, Creon cannot give the same fate to the traitor and the brave: Eteocles died defending his land, but Polyneices died trying to destroy it. For the tyrant, enemies remain enemies forever, even after death. Antigone replies that she was not born to bind herself in hatred, but in love: Polyneices was her brother, not a slave, and Hades requires rites to be performed for all the deceased.

Loyal to the unwritten law of the fraternal bond, Antigone goes to her death.

"The scene between Antigone and Ismene before Creon highlights Antigone's heroic humanity and strength. Ismene is drawn to her higher morality. Indeed, her love for her sister and the awareness of having failed a sacred duty bring Ismene to falsely accuse herself, in an attempt to sacrifice a life that, previously, she feared losing.

Before such love and sincere anguish, at the end of the scene Antigone says harsh and pained words: "Be of good cheer; you live; but my soul has long been given to death, that so I might serve the dead."[6]

Haemon, Antigone's betrothed, uselessly tries to persuade his father Creon to spare the girl: "Father, the gods give reason to men, the highest of all things that we can call our own. It is not for me— far from me be the quest!—to say wherein you err; and yet another man, too, might have some useful thought. [. . .] The dread of your frown forbids citizens from speaking words that would offend your ear; but one can hear murmurs in the dark, of the city for this girl: 'no woman', they say, 'ever deserved her doom less,—none ever was to die so shamefully for deeds so glorious as hers; who, when their own brother has fallen in bloody struggle, would leave him unburied, to be devoured by carrion dogs, or by any bird: deserves not she a golden honor?'"

Antigone is led to her death. Creon sentences her to be sealed alive in a cave. Loyal to her faith in the gods and to her brother, after the tension of rendering due homage to Polyneices and defending her cause, Antigone laments her lost youth and her impending death as the guards take her to the cave where she will die. She is overwhelmed by the anguish of having to die so young, alone, in a moment when she should have been celebrating her nuptials.

---

6   *Ibid.*

With Antigone's exit from the scene, Creon's tragedy begins. The infallible oracle Teiresias tells him of the wrath of the gods, who are indignant that Polyneices' burial was forbidden; he foretells the evils that his edict will bring upon him and upon the city. Creon first resists; then, floored by the threatening visions, ends up acquiescing. He orders Polyneices' burial and Antigone's release. However, it is too late. The Chorus hopelessly invokes the god Dionysius, the protector of Thebes, to save the city from all evil, but a messenger announces that Antigone has killed herself in the cave and that Haemon, seeing her body, has killed himself too. Upon this, Eurydice, Haemon's mother, also commits suicide. Creon then appears with his son's body in his arms: he wails over his ruin and desperately invokes death.

"Antigone is the hero of religious, moral and human duty, which is felt with invincible force. She does not have tender words for Polyneices: her sacrifice is motivated by her love for her descent, by her sense of religion."[7]

Antigone considers it her religious and eternal duty to bury her dead brother and disobey Creon's edict, since he has turned out to be an odious tyrant who has violated divine laws, instead of a supporter of the State's law. Thus, Antigone's rebellion against the decree is legitimate, as she states herself: "it was not Zeus that published that edict; the laws established for men by the justice who dwells with the gods below are not such; nor have I deemed that your decrees were of such force that a mortal could override the unwritten and unfailing statutes of heaven. For their life is not of today or yesterday, but of all time, and no man knows when they were first laid out."

The tragedy thus transcends Polyneices' funeral rites to explore the problem of obedience to the laws enacted by men. It acquires a universal dimension, in its affirmation that the validity of human laws derives from their conformity with divine laws.

"Sophocles was fascinated by man's secular faith and wrote a hymn to celebrate the inventive and organizational capacity of human ingeniousness. Man has conquered the strength of the sea: he knows how to cross it even when tempests are raging; he has broken the land and made it fertile through the skill of ploughing; he has managed to catch birds, fish, wild beasts, and to tame horses and

---

[7] *Ibid.*, p. 133.

bulls; he knows how to use words, he elaborates his thoughts, he has organized social life, and constructed civilization. It appears that he has conquered all obstacles except death, and even here, he has been able to hinder its advance by discovering medicines to cure diseases that were once fatal.

Man is truly sagacious, and knows how to find all sorts of solutions. Man's prodigious abilities concern techniques, but the *Homo faber* does not always coincide with the *Homo sapiens*; if the former is unaware of his limits and raises his *io* to the absolute norm in moral life, he is ruined."[8]

---

[8]   G. Tarditi, *Storia della letteratura greca*, Loescher, 1973, p. 161.

CHAPTER 3

ELEANOR OF ARBOREA

(Molins de Rei, 1340-Oristano, 1404)

Medieval lawmaker who fought for equality and women's rights

The Judge Eleanor of Arborea lived in the second half of the 14th century. She is famous for having enacted a code of laws entitled *Carta de Logu*, which remained in force in most of the island of Sardinia until 1827, with very few amendments.

"In Medieval Sardinia, the "Judges" were independent princes who governed the four zones, called "Judicates", into which the island was divided after the end of Byzantine rule in 827: with the Arab invasion of Sicily, Sardinia was isolated from Byzantium and had therefore to defend itself against Saracen incursions.

At first, there were four Judicates: Torres or Lugodoro in the northwest, Gallura in the northeast, Cagliari or Pluminos in the southwest, and Arborea in the plains surrounding Oristano, along the Tirso valley and the other coastal areas to the west. Arborea had the most fertile land of the entire island, land which consisted of about one-fourth of Sardinia, and had the rich and flourishing city of Oristano as its capital."[9]

Eleanor was born in 1340 to Mariano IV, Judge of Arborea from 1347 to 1376, and Timobra de Roccaberti. The House of Arborea extended its power over one-third of Sardinia, and was the general population's only defense against foreign domination.

Eleanor spent her youth at the court of Arborea (near Oristano), which, under the thirty-year rule of her father, an erudite and

---

[9]   Bianca Pitzorno, *Vita di Eleonora d'Arborea*, Mondadori, Milano, 2010, p. 6.

intelligent man, was lively and refined, with the same atmosphere that characterized most of Europe at that time. Indeed, it was the golden age of Dante, Petrarch and Boccaccio; national languages and literatures were gradually becoming established.

A contemporary of Eleanor was Cristina da Pizzano, the daughter of Tommaso, a doctor and astrologer who was called to the French court of Charles V; she was the first woman to support herself thanks to her own literary skills.

Mariano was succeeded by his son Ugone, Eleanor's brother and a chieftain.

Eleanor had grown up with a natural propensity for weaponry, and was married off to the nobleman Brancaleone Doria (1337-1409). Her marriage was part of a greater plan to form an alliance between the Arborea and the Doria families, who already controlled vast parts of Sardinia, to contrast the Aragon forces. The couple went to live in Castelgenovese (today called Castelsardo), where their sons Federico and Mariano were born.

The marriage guaranteed Sardinia's peace and protection against the Aragon domination, and was welcomed by the population with much jubilation. Ugone, now a Judge, continued to fight against Peter IV of Aragon and the Catalans. This made him some enemies among the local Sardinian nobility, who tried to provoke the poorer classes to rebel.

Displaying great political foresight and a clear vision of her lineage's dynastic future, on 16 September 1382 Eleanor concluded an agreement with the *Doge* (ruler) of the Republic of Genoa, Nicolò di Guarco, who held major interests and property throughout northern Sardinia. According to the terms of the agreement, Nicolò's daughter Bianchina was to marry Federico, Eleanor's eldest son; Eleanor was to give a loan of four thousand gold florins to the Doge, who committed to repaying it within ten years, failing which he would have had to pay double the original amount.

On 3 March 1383, Ugone and his daughter, future heir to the throne, were killed in a conspiracy. Eleanor proclaimed herself *Juighissa de Arbaree*, as ancient royal Sardinian law allowed women to inherit the throne from their father or brother.

"The new Judge knew that the Aragons could not be allowed to pose an obstacle, intent as they were on conquering the whole island, and thus decided to send her husband Brancaleone Doria to Spain, to the Court of Peter IV of Aragon, to promote her will.

Peter IV understood the gravity of the situation. He considered it highly inconvenient to leave such a powerful family in Sardinia, and thus ordered Brancaleone Doria to be kept hostage until his son Federico was handed over to the Spanish king, and until he could force Eleanor into obedience. If not, Peter IV would have set the Aragon army upon the rebels. Brancaleone Doria accepted these terms, but Eleanor preferred a war with the Aragons to an ignominious surrender and to handing over her eldest son. She disobeyed her husband, who begged her from jail to acquiesce."[10]

In the meantime, Eleanor travelled across the whole island to visit the territory's castles and burgs, granting tax exemptions in return for acceptance[11] and firmly intervening to reorganize and expand the Judicate. "She summoned the magistrates, the elders and the entire population of free men and serfs, asking them for an oath of loyalty to her son Federico. The initiative was successful: thousands of soldiers arrived to defend her in the name of justice and of the Sardinian people. The financial resources of the Doria family allowed her to pay officials to train the army.

However, after two years of fruitless battles, Eleanor realized that her obstinacy was condemning her husband to prison. She bribed servants and guards to help him escape the prison of Saint Pancras in Cagliari, but one of these informed the governor and her plan failed.

She began to negotiate a peace treaty, but King Peter IV of Aragon died during the negotiations.

In the same year, 1387, her firstborn son Federico also died. His brother Mariano V succeeded him, under the regency of Eleanor.

The second peace treaty was more onerous than the first, and was signed only one year after the death of the King. However, one whole year will elapse before Brancaleone Doria was freed after seven years of prison. War broke out in Sardinia once again: on 1 March 1392,

---

10   Verena Mantovani. "Eleonora d'Arborea" *Enciclopedia delle donne*, www.enciclopediadelledonne.it.

11   Pitzorno, *op. cit.*, p. 260.

Eleanor and her husband were accused of rebellion and perjury, and were sentenced to death.

Further talks of peace treaties occasionally arose, and ambassadors travelled between Cagliari and Oristano to discuss proposals (and devise plots).

For Eleanor, it was time to re-establish peace and order. Guided by a strong sense of history, she amended the law to reflect contemporary needs. In 1392, she enacted the new *Carta de Logu* (Law of the Judicate), divided into 198 chapters. The legal document was to remain engraved into the Island's history and will regulate the legal and social lives of the Sardinian people for the next four centuries."[12]

The Code had been originally issued "with great sense and foresight by the judge Mariano[13], our father" wrote Eleanor in the Preamble. Her version was passed sixteen years after its last review; in the meantime, however, the times had changed, and the dispositions of men "had become more inclined to do evil than to do good". Thus, well aware that "the prosperity of the provinces, of the kingdoms and of the lands depends on reason and on the observance of justice, which, through fear of punishments restrains the evil and allows the good, innocent and pure, who love virtue, to live safe among criminals, *Nos Elionora, per issa gratia de dues juiguysa de Arbore, comitissa de Gociani e biscontissa de basso*, we have decided with pondered counsel to correct and change *dae bene in megius* the laws issued by our fathers."[14]

The *Carta de Logu* regulated civil, criminal and administrative legal relationships and sought to enshrine the principle of the equality of all citizens before the law, thereby ensuring the certainty of law. The measures to protect women, children and land, and those against usury, were especially innovative and modern. The *Carta de Logu* was to be a decisive milestone for the implementation of the "rule of law", of a State where all individuals are obliged to observe the law, which was public and thus cognizable. Indeed, thanks to the *Carta*,

---

[12] Mantovani, *op. cit.*

[13] Judge Mariano IV, Eleanor's father, had promulgated a written code of laws, to enable the population to administrate its own affairs with justice and free from the laws of the powerful. The *Carta de Burgos* is Mariano's first legal document.

[14] Pitzorno, *op. cit.*, 321.

all citizens and foreigners could learn the law and the consequences of disobedience.

One of the Code's most important aspects is its drafting in the Sardinian language, with the specific aim of enabling the general population to understand its content.

"Eleanor introduced concepts that were legally advanced for her times, and certainly very modern. She established that all men were equal before the law (in the 1300s!), that the same penalty was to be imposed upon all those who violated the law, regardless of social class; this was a revolutionary concept for those times. She emphasized the value of the subjective aspect of crime, distinguishing between those who killed *con animo delliberadu e pensadamenti* (deliberately and with intention) and those who killed without intention.

The *Carta* regulates the burning of grass stubble, which is a cause of very serious fires in Sardinia to this day, providing that stubble had to be burnt before the 8th of September. Wills are also provided for: since culture was rather scarce in her Judicature and there were no notaries, Eleanor empowered parish priests and scribes to receive wills, so as to ensure the observance of the wishes of the deceased. The *Carta* also punished assault, theft, usury, deceit and judicial negligence; it regulates the deposition of witness statements, adverse possession, hunting, livestock rearing, tax matters, trade, and all issues related to the legal, administrative and social life of the judicature"[15].

The *Carta de Logu* consisted of a Preamble and 198 Chapters, the first 132 were devoted to the Civil and Penal Code; the remaining 66 constituted the Rural Code, issued by Mariano IV of Arborea in 1353.

The 198 Chapters are divided thus:
I-XVI: the crimes of "lèse-majesté", homicide, suicide and assault and battery.
XVII-XLIV: *Ordinamentos de furas e de maleficios* (various kinds of theft, rape, loans, debts and perjury).
XLV-XLIX: *Ordinamentos de foghu* (fire regulations on the burning of grass stubble, fields etc.).

---

15   Mantovani, *op. cit.*

15

L-LXXX: *Ordinamentos de chertos e de nunzas* (provisions on disputes and suits).

LXXXI-CV: *Ordinamentos de silvas* (provisions on hunting, fishing, protecting land and water fauna, horsemen and their horses, family law).

CVI-CXI: *Ordinamentos de corgios et de mercantes* (provisions on leather processing, firebranding and the leather trade).

CXII-CXXIII: *Ordinamentos de sa guardia de sus laores, vingnas et ortos* (provisions for protecting cereal crops, the fencing of vineyards and agricultural fields, against trespassing animals, and establishing festive days).

CXXIV-CXXXII: *Ordinamentos de salarios* (miscellaneous provisions on issues ranging from the salaries of judges and other royal figures, to punishments for blasphemy etc.)

CXXXIII-CLIX: *Ordinamentos de vignas, de lavores e de ortos* (provisions on vineyards, cereal crops and agricultural fields).

CLX-CXCVIII: *Ordinamentos de cumonis, de maxellos, de terminis e iniurias* (provisions on limited partnerships, butchery, boundaries and "defamation").

We can thus see that Eleanor sought to confirm the State's power, to protect religiousness and to defend women (in particular) and the family (in general).

"Child orphans whose parents had died were entrusted to a guardian, chosen by the local authority, from among the child's closest relatives or strangers of good reputation. The individual chosen as guardian could not turn down the charge without a satisfactory reason. A copy of the inventory of the ward's possessions was to be filed with the Judicature's Registry, which reserved the power to check the guardian's behavior and to defend the child's interests. Also, no descendants, whether adult or child, could be excluded from the inheritance process without a legitimate reason; daughters enjoyed the same inheritance rights as sons."[16]

In Arborea, as in the rest of the island, falconry was widespread. Sardinia's falcons were well-known throughout Europe, and were so valuable that they were even sought by foreign royalty. The judges of Arborea held a monopoly over them or extended their use, as a

---

[16] Pitzorno, *op. cit.*, p. 332.

special privilege, to particularly deserving vassals. The *Carta de Logu* banned all individuals from removing chicks or young falcons from their nests for training them for personal use. The punishment for violating these provisions was comparable to that reserved for the most serious crimes, such as homicide.

Eleanor, as all members of her family, enjoyed falconry, which was moreover the only hunting activity considered becoming to women at the time. In this connection, it may be interesting to note that in 1839, the French ornithologist Gené gave the name of "Falco eleonorae" to a new falcon species that lives along the northwestern coasts of Sardinia[17].

"Article 21 concerns rape. It established two principles which are extraordinarily advanced, even in relation to modern legislation. According to the first principle, marriage could redress the wrong only if the woman approved of the man ("*si est senca maridu e plaquiat asa femina*"), and in any case was not full reparation as the guilty party also had to choose between paying a very high fine to the State (equivalent to the value of twenty battlehorses!), or have a foot cut off. If the woman did not want the man as a husband, the rapist was still obliged to provide for her future with a dowry that was suitable to her social status, such that she could marry another man. This too did not exempt him from the further condition of choosing between the fine or having a foot cut off[18]. The punishment was the same regardless of whether the woman was nubile or already betrothed ("*bagadja o jurada*").

Moreover, compatibly with the times, accused individuals enjoyed very broad defense rights which were entirely inconceivable in feudal times. "The summons, '*sa nunca*', had to be personally delivered in the presence of witnesses, and the messenger had to search for the charged individual three times—always recording his actions—if

---

[17]   The species' scientific name is *Falco eleonorae*, in honor of Eleanor of Arborea. In her code, she had included an article that banned hunting for adult falcons and nestlings. The species' ordinary names in the main languages of the world all recall Eleanor except, strangely enough, for Italian (Italian: *falco della regina*; English: Eleanor's falcon; French: *faucon d'Eléonore*; Spanish: *halcón de Eleonor*; German: *Eleonorenfalke*; http://it.wikipedia.org/wiki/Falco_della_regina).

[18]   Pitzorno, pp. 329-330.

17

he did not find him. During the trial, '*su chertu*', the defendant was entitled to legal defense and could name up to ten (adult) witnesses to support his version. He could not be tortured to extract a confession, unless he already had a bad reputation. Judgment was not entrusted to one person alone, but to a panel of *boni homines*, of good men, which was not as easily influenced by personal enmities or bribery. If the panel found against the defendant, the latter could appeal twice.

These procedures may seem obvious today, but for the times were greatly innovative. Also, Eleanor is often recalled as one of the first lawmakers to establish the crime of misfeasance and the condition of reciprocity in dealing with foreigners."[19]

In 1421, the Spanish dominators extended the applicability of the *Carta de Logu* throughout Sardinia. It remained in force, with few amendments, until the enactment of the Albertine Statutes of 1827. Previous legal texts became obsolete (such as Cagliari's *Carta de Logu*) or only locally applicable, such as the Iglesias *Breve* and the statutes of Sassari.

"According to historians, this happened thanks to the *Carta*'s intrinsic worth, for its contents which were rich with legal knowledge, as well as thanks to its perfect reflection of the island's social reality; these features made the *Carta* one of the highest and enduring testaments of Sardinian civilization."[20]

Eleanor died of plague in 1404, three years before the death of Mariano V, who neither married nor had children, and was succeeded by William III. With Eleanor's death, Arborea slowly fell into decline, and ended in 1420 with the Spanish invasion of Sardinia.

Even after sixty years, Sardinia had not been able to escape the Aragons and finally succumbed, becoming a Spanish dominion. Nothing remained of the ancient Judicature of Arborea, of its civilization and of its dreams of independence—nothing, except Eleanor's Code.

---

[19]   *Ibid.*, pp. 334-335
[20]   *Ibid.*, p. 335.

CHAPTER 4

THE SUFFRAGETTES

Women's vote and more

Between the late 1700s and the early 1800s, women began to aspire to obtain the rights granted to men. In 1787, two years before the French Revolution, the two American women Mercy Otis Warren and Abigail Adams lay the foundations for the women's suffrage movement in the United States. Intellectual women from all social and popular classes took an active part in the movements throughout the world. In Paris, Etta Palms, Madame de Keralis, and Olympia de Gouges had started women's clubs (*Société fraternelle, Société des femmes révolutionnaires*, and others). The women of the *Troisième État* draft the first manifestos: Madame de Keralis presents the *Cahier des doléances et reclamations des femmes* to the Revolutionary Assembly, a text which can be considered as the first claim to women's rights in history. The document called for "the admission of all female persons to the assemblies regardless [of their gender] . . . , their election to municipal offices and to the National Assembly if they fulfil the conditions required by the electoral law. Women must be able to vote in consultative and deliberative decisions."

On June 3rd, 1792, women were admitted to a national ceremony, "the festival of law", and to the commemoration of the storming of the Bastille on July 14th of that year.

Olympe de Gouges was a fervent defender of women's rights. She drafted the Declaration of the Rights of Woman and of the Female Citizen, based on the 1789 Declaration of the Rights of Man and of the [Male] Citizen. In her document, she affirmed the equality of civil and political rights between the two sexes and insisted that women be returned their natural rights, which had been removed from them by the strength of prejudice. In those times, eligibility to vote was based on social status (for a worker, the mere act of going to vote entailed the loss of three working days), and the majority of the French population simply could not afford it. Olympe called for the introduction of divorce (which was allowed soon after the Revolution), and fought for the freedom to learn one's paternity and to recognize children born out of wedlock. She was one of the first promoters of a welfare system, broadly devising a system to protect mothers and children, and recommended the establishment of national measures to fight unemployment; Olympe also proposed the creation of shelters for beggars and the poor.

On December 16, 1792, Olympe de Gouges offered to help the French jurist and politician Malesherbes to defend the King in the trial before the revolutionary authorities, but was turned down. Olympe ceaselessly argued that women were fully capable of assuming all traditionally "male" responsibilities, and called for women to be allowed to participate in political and social debates. In her Declaration of the Rights of Woman, she wrote "if women have the right to tread the gallows, they must also have the right to tread in court".

In 1793, Olympe prosecuted the individuals responsible for the atrocities committed on September 2 and 3, 1792, including Marat. She suspected that Robespierre aspired to become a dictator and issued several writings in which she questioned him; these eventually cost her a lawsuit before the Jacobins. Her positions led her to be arrested and brought before the Revolutionary Tribunal on August 6, 1793; she was executed during the Terror.

Contemporary witness accounts state that Olympe went to her death with great courage and dignity. However, the prosecutor of the City of Paris Pierre-Gaspard Chaumette taunted her statements and expressed satisfaction at her execution; he believed that she deserved it, because she "had forgotten the virtues befitting her gender".

In 1793, despite Condorcet's impassioned defense, the Committee of National Security rejected the claims advanced by women and women's organizations during the Revolution. On October 28th, 1793, Robespierre ordered women's clubs to be dissolved.

In the wake of the French Revolution's influence, feminist ideals had spread to England: in 1792, Mary Wollstonecraft published *A Vindication of the Rights of Woman*.

This was Wollstonecraft's most important work, a corollary of her treatise *A Vindication of the Rights of Men*, and one of the first writings to expound feminist theory.

Wollstonecraft posited that women must receive an education appropriate for their social position; all women are essential for their nation, since they educate their children and are—or could be— "companions" to their husbands and not merely "wives". Instead of a social ornament and an "object of sale" in the context of marriage, insofar as women are human beings, they too enjoy the fundamental rights granted to men. Through this aspect of her ideology, Wollstonecraft sharply critiqued James Fordyce, John Gregory and Jean-Jacques Rousseau, who denied women's right to education: in *Émile* (published in 1762), Rousseau had argued that women should only receive the education necessary for pleasing men.

Wollstonecraft noticed that the women of her times were often frivolous and superficial, and blamed this on the failure to give them a proper education. "Taught from their infancy, that beauty is woman's scepter, the mind shapes itself to the body, and, roaming round its gilt cage, only seeks to adorn its prison"; they would be capable of much loftier goals if only they were not encouraged to pay so much attention to their appearance.

Before the *Vindication of the Rights of Woman*, Wollstonecraft had written *Thoughts on the education of daughters: with reflections on female conduct, in the more important duties of life*, her first work, published in 1787 by her friend Joseph Johnson. This was a conduct book, which provided advice on the education of girls and was directed especially to the nascent British middle class. Although it mainly covered issues of morality and etiquette, it also featured basic suggestions for educating girls and caring for infants. Wollstonecraft encouraged mothers to teach their daughters critical thinking and self-discipline, and to instil in them the values of honesty, adaptability and *savoir faire*, all useful tools in dealing with life. The book taught young girls how to become industrious women and mothers who would be comfortable in the adult world, and could effectively contribute to the advancement of society.

British 19ᵗʰ-century conduct books proliferated enormously in the second half of that century, deriving from the older literary traditions of advice manuals and religious precepts. Wollstonecraft's work, however, enjoyed only moderate success: it obtained one review and was reprinted only once, other than being published in some popular periodicals of the time. It was then republished only in the 1970s, when the European feminist movement developed and began to trace its history.

In 1850, the first feminist conventions in America were held in New York and Worcester. The movements claimed full civil and political rights for women, including the right to vote and to run as candidates in elections.

In 1865, the first women's associations in Germany were created (in Lipsia and Berlin), to fight for work-related civil and economic rights.

However, the real "suffragette" movement has its roots in the United Kingdom. In 1897, Millicent Fawcett founded the National Union of Women's Suffrage, a national movement for the vindication of women's rights, in which she encouraged the participation of men too. Millicent Fawcett had two daughters, Christabel and Sylvia, who continued her cause.

The suffragette movement gained publicity in the early 1900s, following Emmeline Pankhurst's arrest for protesting for women's rights near Buckingham Palace. She supported several groups, especially the Women's Franchise League, and in 1894, she succeeded in gaining women's right to vote in local elections. In 1903 Pankhurst founded the Women's Social and Political Union, with the aim of extending women's right to vote in all elections. The movement claimed to be politically independent, but had gained a negative reputation due to the suffragettes' violent actions, which often damaged public buildings.

In 1918, Pankhurst won the women's right to vote in elections to the House of Commons.

In the same year, the English Parliament granted the right to vote to wives of heads of families over the age of 30. Nancy Astor was the first woman elected to Parliament in England, on November 1ˢᵗ,

1919, for the Conservative Party. However, truly universal suffrage was achieved only in 1928.

From 1869, groups similar to the English suffragettes began to form in the United States too, with the establishment of the National Association for Women's Suffrage. The State of Wyoming was the first to grant women the vote[21].

In 1920, the Congress approved the XIX Amendment to the Constitution of the United States of America: "The right of citizens of the United States to vote shall not be denied or abridged by the United States or by any state on account of sex."

In Germany, women obtained the right in 1919.

"In 1901 the Australian Federation recognized the principle of the equality of women's political rights. Australia was thus the first country where women's vote was achieved, and all gender distinctions in the Constitution and ordinary legislation abolished."[22]

In 1907, women obtained the right to vote in Finland (the first country in Europe).

"In 1945, in Europe and Asia new legal and political rights were acquired by women in Poland, Hungary, Yugoslavia, Germany, France and Japan"[23].

In 1946 the rights to vote and to be elected in administrative and political elections were obtained in Italy. The Constitution of the Italian Republic expressly enshrines the full equality of the rights of men and women.

Switzerland granted universal suffrage only in 1971.

---

[21] The first country in the world to recognize universal women's suffrage was New Zealand, in 1823.

[22] A. Valle and A. Coviello, *Anch'io ho votato Repubblica*, Edizioni Giacché, La Spezia p. 168.

[23] *Ibid.*, p. 170.

CHAPTER 5

BERTHA von SUTTNER

(Prague, 9 June 1843-Vienna, 21 June 1914)

Lay down your arms, and spread the word!

"War must stop and all must contribute all they can, so that humanity can approach this goal, even by one-thousandth of a line".

"Peace is the greatest benefit or, rather, the absence of the greatest calamity is the only condition that can enable the interests of nations to prosper".

"O, tomorrow! . . . tomorrow! . . . A sea of fire,
Which, with its flaming waves,
Threatens to swallow that entire family!
The sword was a symbol of war and, with firm
Grasp, it gave to the victor bounty
And glory . . . Today War uses other weapons
Both volcano and dust!—Ruthless,
And furious, and blind, of one
With skeptical fury,
Does not bring glory to those who win; to the defeated it brings
Only harm; and for all, calamity!"
(from the Prologue recited at Nuremberg, 1896)

Bertha von Suttner was born in Prague on 9 June 1843, to an Austrian family. Her father was Count Francis Kinsky, an Austrian marshal who had fought at the battle of Custoza under General Radetzky, and her mother was young Sophia Wilhelmine von Korner, a poet who was related to the poet Theodore Korner. Bertha was still a child when her father died; despite suffering financial hardships, her mother lovingly took charge of her daughter's education and appointed two governesses, one French and one English, who taught her those two languages. Bertha also had a flair for singing. In 1876 she left Vienna and, answering a vacancy, gained a job in Paris as secretary to the scientist Alfred Nobel. Soon later, at the age of thirty-three, she married the Baron and writer Arthur Gundaccar von Suttner, who was seven years her junior: the wedding took place against their families' will.

The couple initially moved to the Caucasus region, accepting the hospitality of the Princess of Mingrelia. Some time later, they decided to earn their living while travelling throughout the southern provinces of Russia. Arthur taught drawing and worked as an engineer; Bertha taught singing and foreign languages and literature. In 1884, Bertha and Arthur reconciled with the von Suttner family and began to live in the Harmansdorf castle, fifty kilometers from Vienna. Bertha von Suttner zealously devoted herself to the campaign for universal peace; in 1864 she had participated in the International Conference of Geneva organized by Henry Dunant, who, during the 1859 battle of Solferino, was deeply impressed by the women who nursed the suffering men, regardless of their provenance.

At the Conference, Henry Dunant, the supporter of the Red Cross, proclaimed the neutrality of individuals injured in war, and promoted the foundation of the Help Society.

Baron von Suttner enthusiastically embraced his wife's pacifist ideals. In 1883, Bertha wrote her first novel, "Inventory of a soul", inspired by Nobel's dream of constructing ever-more terrifying war weaponry that could render any traditional war strategy vain. Nobel himself stated:

". . . on the day that two army corps can mutually annihilate each other in a second, all civilized nations will surely recoil with horror and disband their troops."

In 1889, Bertha wrote her second novel, "The Time Macine", where she detailed her critique of a society too strongly oriented towards nationalism and armament. The same year, she published the work that will bring her international fame, "*Lay down your arms!*", a love story that discusses the tragedy of war.

"Bertha is in Paris. In the press stand, there are journalists, politicians, publishers and others. Bertha gives a speech on the need to foster brotherhood, to abandon the hurried rush to arms in which governments appear to compete ever more—in other words, to reach universal peace through love and friendship, and not through the enduring sacrifice of so much human blood.

This is the content of my manuscript "Lay down your arms", that I would like to publish. What do you think?

Her addressees looked at each other. Most wore a perplexed expression, others smiled ironically; timid, isolated claps could be heard, but the mood remained chilly. Bertha looked disappointed and tired. But from the far corner of the room, a calm, sharp voice spoke. It came from a seat at the very end of one of the last, almost empty, rows.

Ladies and gentlemen, your restraint proves, unfortunately, that the highest and most profound truths are fated to be misunderstood and to struggle with prejudices and banality. Madam Bertha von Suttner's ideas are not only highly noble on a human level, but are also the only path to safety for humanity.

Everyone turned towards the voice. A small, tired-looking man, with gray hair and beard, subtly dressed, is the speaker.

Whispers quickly started to spread and a fascinating name was murmured among the eminent crowd.

It's Nobel.

No, it can't be.

Of all people, *he* could not possibly approve these theories!

Yes, it's Nobel . . . Nobel . . .

The name bounced from person to person, circulates, and eventually the entire audience hung from his lips with a respectful, eager expression, while Bertha's face, silent and touched, betrayed her intimate and deep emotion.

Nobel continued:

Yes, ladies and gentlemen, I, although animated by a spirit of progress and peace, have unintentionally provided weapons ever more lethal, for destruction and war. Although my conscience is clear, I feel that I have expiated, and must yet expiate, these tremendous applications of my discovery, with solitude, doubt, the bitterness of a futile glory and a wealth paid with the blood of the innocent. I therefore bow down to this woman who has sacrificed her youth and beauty to the sublime dream of peace and love.

I am convinced that the possession of more perfect weapons by all nations is a practical and powerful means to maintain peace. But I am even more firmly convinced that the peaceful union of all peoples, the dawn of a future society, will rise from the flame lit by the small hands of this woman, whose name will one day be honored among those of the greatest benefactors of our destiny.

Needless to say, the publishers in the room had realized that Bertha's initiative enjoyed the prestigious support of such a powerful figure as Nobel. They ran to Bertha's table, arguing and fighting over the honor of publishing the book that they had just rejected.

"Lay down your arms" was a triumphant success of Bertha's ideas, and was published in eight languages.

The vast hall in Bern, Switzerland, was full of people. Bertha had taken the stage; amidst complete silence, she finished her speech at the first World Peace Congress. A loud, lengthy ovation met her concluding words, and she was visibly touched.

Alfred Nobel had inconspicuously entered the hall, listening in a corner. When the applause began, he quietly left.

Some time later, Alfred retired to his villa in San Remo. One winter morning, his generous heart laid to rest forever.

The following inscription was sculpted on his tombstone:

"10 December 1896—Alfred Nobel dies in this villa in San Remo. His spirit lives on in the legacy he has left us all: his testament."

"I dispose of my property thus: every year, a prize is to be awarded to those who have performed the greatest service to humanity in the fields of physics, chemistry, medicine, literature and peace among peoples."[24]

Bertha had been the one to suggest Nobel to establish a prize for peace.

Bertha's novel was extraordinarily successful from the day of its publication: in Germany alone it was published 31 times and was translated into several languages, reaching even czarist Russia and militaristic Japan. To think that the manuscript of *Lay Down Your*

---

[24] Nicola Sinopoli, *Una donna per la pace*. Fratelli Palombi Editore, Rome, 1986, pp. 41-44.

Arms! had been rejected by so many publishers, in fear of the possible reaction among political and military circles! The novel's success was ensured also thanks to the praise lavished by famous personalities of the time, such as Alfred Nobel and Leo Tolstoy. The latter told Bertha of his enthusiasm for her work:

"The publishing of your book is, in my opinion, a good sign. The novel *Uncle Tom's Cabin* contributed to abolishing slavery. May God let your book do the same for the abolition of war".

The book was written in the form of an autobiography. The protagonist, also born in a traditionally militaristic environment, has much in common with the author. As probably happened for Bertha, Martha's hatred of war and her aspiration for an ideal of peace unfurls slowly, as she observes the world around her; as she perceives the detachment between popular depictions of war, described from afar, and its horrors clear upon first-hand experience, its destruction of the holiest bonds, its transformation of man into brute for a putative sentiment of honor and duty. War thrusts humanity back into its days of savagery.

"In my diary I find some of my own thoughts, expressed in those times by a very young author, Guy de Maupassant, who later gained great fame:

War! At the mere mention of the word, I am seized with a sense of bewilderment, as though I heard of witchcraft, of the inquisition, of some far distant thing, ended long ago, abominable and monstrous, against all natural law. War! Fighting! Slaughtering! Butchering Men! And to think that now, in our own century, with all our civilization, with the expansion of science and the height of philosophy to which the human race is supposed to have attained, we should have schools in which we teach the art of killing, of killing from afar, to perfection, numbers of people at the same time . . . The most astounding thing is that the people do not rise up against the governing power . . . bodily in rebellion at the word "war" . . .

Whosoever governs must consider it as much his duty to avoid war as it is that of the captain of a vessel to avoid shipwreck. When a captain has lost his ship, he is judged and condemned if found guilty of negligence or even of incapacity. Why should not governments be judged after the declaration of every war? If the people understood this, if they took the law into their own hands against the murdering powers, if they refused to allow themselves to be killed without a reason [. . .] That day indeed war would be a dead letter.

In the same period, Ernest Renan too wrote on the subject:

Is it not dismaying to think that all we men of science and study have toiled to produce in these fifty years, is about to be wiped out in a single stroke: goodwill between peoples, mutual knowledge and understanding of nations, their efforts, so powerful, in all fields. War kills the love for truth: how much slander, how many lies will be avidly said and believed from people to people! What an obstacle to the path of European progress! Ah! We will be powerless to raise up again, in one hundred years' time, that which war is about to destroy in a single day!"[25]

"Due to the gaps in European historiography, we are unaware of the significance of the pacifist movement and of the respect shown to the calls to peace issued by the leaders of the great demonstrations and congresses to the European sovereigns, in the late 19th—and early 20th centuries. The pacifism of the time was characterized by a strong utopian tension, but also by fervid support for its translation into democratic and legal constructs: Bertha belonged to the latter school of thought.

However, even the most reasonable efforts were defeated by the decisive, ultimate, power of traditional military structures and war ministries, and of the interests deemed non-negotiable for national pride. Even less discernible is the importance of the presence of women in defending peace—a peace that neither then nor now was successfully enshrined in a right. Indeed, women were more sensitive to the pacifist cause and Bertha, who quickly understood their potential, expressed her solidarity to the movements for women's rights.

Bertha, defined by the chauvinistic press of her time as "the witch of peace", and who was mocked in atrocious satirical vignettes, spared no effort: "Women will not be quiet. We will write, we will hold speeches, we will work, we will act. Women will change society and themselves"[26].

---

[25] *Ibid.*, pp. 126-128.

[26] Giancarla Codrignani, "Bertha von Suttner". *Enciclopedia delle donne*, www. enciclopediadelledonne.it.

The Baroness wrote many more campaign articles, and travelled around Europe and America to spread the ideals of the pacifist movement, holding many conferences in the main North American cities[27].

Her influence could be felt in the Hague Conference and the Hamburg Congress, in Geneva, Rome, Paris, London, New York[28].

In 1891, Bertha founded the Austrian Society for Peace, of which she was the President until her death. In the same year, she spoke at the Conference for Peace held in Rome, on the Capitol hill: it was the first time for a woman to speak in a place of such historical value, and the first time for Bertha to speak in an official event, before a vast and demanding audience. Still, she performed brilliantly; even the ill-disposed Roman journalists, who had spared no irony on the woman who dared speak to an audience of men, in such a solemn setting, were forced to admit the reasonableness of her ideas and her passion in supporting them.

From 1892, Bertha worked on the monthly publication "Lay down your arms!", which echoed the title and spirit of her most famous book. A young publisher, Alfred Hermann Fried, who went on to win the Nobel Peace Prize in 1911, helped her in her efforts. Here—and on "The Peace Watchtower" that will replace it in 1899—Bertha von Suttner published her famous "notes to the history of time", a polemical column that infuriated the nationalistic and imperialistic circles of all Europe. In spite of attacks and derision by war supporters, in 1892 "the witch of peace" and her collaborator A. H. Fried founded the German Society for Peace in Berlin.

Her writings and speeches turned out to be exceptionally prophetic: at the 1892 Fourth World Congress for Peace held in Bern, von Suttner, the only female delegate, presented a report on a project for a Confederation of the States of Europe.

---

27 "Last year, Bertha went to America, visiting the main cities and holding conferences, which aroused the greatest admiration" (article that appeared on the daily newspaper *Il Secolo* on June 22, 1914).

28 "Bertha von Suttner was a lady endowed with great culture and intelligence. Moreover, she possessed an easy and elegant eloquence, and these qualities led to making her…a veritable apostle for universal peace" (article written by Giovanni Galluzzi ang published on the daily newspaper *Corriere della sera* on 22 June 1914).

At the Peace Conference held in The Hague in 1899, the first which will enjoy the participation of state and government figures of several countries, she stated that "the 20ᵗʰ century will not end without society abolishing as a legal institution the greatest of scourges—war"[29].

The situation in Europe was increasingly complex. On one hand, the Baroness followed the continent's issues, working for peace between potentially rival countries (she contributed to the creation of the Anglo-German Committee of Brotherhood); on the other she perceived—and denounced—the deterioration of international tensions. She also drew attention to the dangers posed by technological advances in weapon production.

Her renown crossed the Atlantic Ocean: in 1904, only two years after the death of her beloved husband, she held over one hundred conferences in the United States. She was received by President Theodore Roosevelt, and persuaded him to promote the Second Hague Peace Conference (1907), which established the Permanent Court of Arbitration. Bertha received the 1905 Nobel Peace Prize for her efforts; she was the first woman to receive it.

Bjornson, a member of the Committee awarding the Nobel Peace Prizes said in his speech:

"*We thank you, Madam Baroness, for your steadfast faith, your hope, your sacrifice and your work. We too, in the lands of northern Europe, women and men, need you to light and nurture the flame of faith and work. All the best to you!*"

Indefatigable, Bertha convinced Andrew Carnegie, one of the greatest exponents of North American enlightened capitalism, to create a foundation for peace. However, her work is a desperate race against time: public opinion in all European countries is infused with an ever-firmer will to war. In an essay, "The barbarity of the air" (1912), Bertha, with a lucidly utopian vision, understood and denounced with much advance the radically new and atrocious ways of conceiving and practicing war.

Sadly, the terrible bombings that took place thirty years later fulfilled Bertha's dark prophecies. Fate however spared her from

---

[29]   In 1912, General Giulio Douhet (1869-1930), a theorist of air warfare and strategic aviation, published his book entitled "The Command of the Air".

witnessing the horrors of World War I: she died on 21 June 1914, one week before the Sarajevo shooting finally precipitated the European tensions, and while the preparations for the Vienna World Peace Conference, yet another pacifist initiative inspired by this formidable woman, were in full swing. Bertha von Suttner had foreseen the explosion of World War I before and better than the sovereigns, statesmen and armed forces, and would have certainly fought for the adoption of preventive policies.

Baroness von Suttner said her last words a few minutes before her death. They were noted by her sister-in-law: "Lay down your arms! Tell it to all!"

Bertha von Suttner's extraordinary personality and activity influenced much of the literary, cultural and political life of the late 19th and early 20th centuries. The novelty of this extraordinary woman's generous initiative lay in her proposal of a democratic and "legal" pacifism, that placed its faith in the enlightened work of governments and "great" men, rather than in mass and popular uprisings. Today, institutions such as the United Nations, which use agreements and treaties for disarmament, the aversion against the culture of violence and war and the idea of an "education to peace" appear to confirm the soundness of many of her intuitions.

Nobel's armed peace implied a potential for destruction that, by leading to the elimination of armies, endangered all humanity and entailed a waste of resources and energies that could be used for other purposes. Instead, Bertha's solution proposed the total disarmament of all nations and the institution of a court of arbitration to resolve international conflicts, through resort to law and not violence.

Austria chose Bertha von Suttner's portrait for its 2 Euro coin, to commemorate Austria's decades-long efforts towards peace. In this case too, the symbol was chosen by a national group of experts, after a public survey. The artist Joseph Kaiser created the image.

"The most surprising thing, it seems to me, is that men can place themselves alone, voluntarily, in such a state; that men who have seen similar things do not fall to their knees, giving the most impassioned oath to wage war upon war, and, if they are Kings or Princes, do not throw down their swords and, if they do not hold power, do not at least devote their words, writings, thoughts, teachings and actions to one goal: lay down your arms!"

CHAPTER 6

EGLANTYNE JEBB

(Ellesmere, Shropshire 1876-Geneva 1928)

The woman who "Save(d) the Children"

"The salvation of children across the world is not an inherent impossibility. This becomes impossible only if we refuse to achieve it."
"The problem is not lack of money but attitude of mind . . . the world is not ungenerous but unimaginative and very busy."

In the early 20th century, children were still thought of only in relation to the adult world; they were "incomplete" adults, rather than persons with their own specific affective, psychological and intellectual needs. The only special measure regarding children concerned their entry into the labor market.

"However, in the early 1900s something changed, and children receive much more attention. In 1900, the pedagogue Ellen Key proposed dedicating the new century to the welfare of children. Eight years later, the Liberal Party in England approved the first official legal document, the *Children Act*, also known as the "Children's Charter"; this created Child Courts, introduced a registry of parents willing to take custody of children, prohibited children from working in dangerous occupations and raised the minimum age for capital punishment to sixteen. Local authorities also had the power to remove poor children from homeless shelters and to protect them from abuse; eventually, social services and orphanages too were established. As a social worker in Cambridge, Eglantyne Jebb was influenced by these social policies, as well as by the New Liberals' nascent ideas on active citizenship.

The idea of extending citizenship to children was gaining currency, but with the first signs of the Great War, a new international interest occupied her priorities. War and its consequences not only prompted a common awareness of the universal vulnerability of children before such a disaster, but also invested children with a new symbolic potential: they constituted a new generation of citizens and ambassadors of future peaceful international relations. It is precisely between 1919 and 1922 that the first international conventions for the protection of children were signed, thanks to the work of the International Labour Organization, an agency of the Society of Nations, that Eglantyne admired enormously."[30]

Eglantyne Jebb also anticipated the (then) revolutionary idea that children enjoyed particular rights, distinct from those of adults. Eglantyne was also aware than children are particularly vulnerable, in physical and psychological terms, to abuse and negligence. She begins to engage institutions, advancing audacious claims and using unconventional methods to raise public awareness and funds. Eglantyne understood that rights provide the basis for respect, protection and compensation, and in the absence of a specific declaration of their rights, children risked being entirely absent from adults' priorities.

Eglantyne was born in Ellesmere, in Shropshire, England, on 25 August 1876. Her family was affluent and deeply involved in the community. Her father, Arthur Trevor Jebb, was a lawyer and landowner. Her mother, Louisa Eglantyne, had founded the Home Arts and Industries Association to support traditional rural and artisanship activities, which were threatened by the expansion of industrialization and urbanization. Her sister Louise had contributed to the foundation of the *Women's Land Army* during World War I, which organized the farming activities of women; indeed, these had taken the place of their husbands, who had gone to war.

Eglantyne received a degree in Modern History at the University of Oxford and taught in elementary schools for one year. She moved to Cambridge to help her mother, working with the *Charity Organization Society*, which performed charity work according to

---

[30] Clare Mulley, *"The woman who saved the children"*, a Biography of Eglantyne Jebb, founder of Save the Children, Oneworld, Oxford, 2009, p. 304.

rational and modern methods. Eglantyne could scientifically study the best ways to help people. In 1906 she published *Cambridge, a Study in Social Questions.*

As World War I began, with her sister Dorothy, she wrote the *Notes from the foreign press* for the *Cambridge Magazine.* When the War ended, on that same magazine she published some foreign news articles that described the serious consequences of the embargo imposed by the British Government upon the defeated enemies, Austria and Germany. The embargo prohibited any aid to be given to those countries, and its children were dying of hunger[31].

In the same year, Eglantyne was arrested in Trafalgar Square for distributing leaflets with pictures of starved Austrian children. Some of these leaflets can still be seen in the *Save the Children* association's archives. The Government hoped that the arrest would stop this woman, who, thanks to influential friends such as Lord Parmoor and John Maynard Keynes, had been lobbying successfully. Eglantyne defended herself in court by invoking morality. She was declared guilty, but was only fined £5 without costs, which was—as she wrote to her mother—"tantamount to victory". And, for her great satisfaction, and the amusement and joy of her friends who were there to give her moral support, during a break between hearings Archibald Bodkin, the prosecution's chief adviser, gave her his personal support. Indeed, he even donated the symbolic £5 of Eglantyne's fine to her cause. It was one of the first donations to a new emergency help fund for children. Indeed, on 15 April 1919, Eglantyne and her sister Dorothy established an aid fund for German and Austrian children: the *Save the Children Fund.*

The organization, presented at the Royal Albert Hall on 19 May 1919, unexpectedly raises a large sum of money from the British public in little time, and many participate in the aid work. To manage the Fund, Eglantyne guaranteed that she would use the professional methods learnt during her work for the *Charity Organization Society.* In summer 1919, she wrote to Pope Benedict XV to ask for the Church's support in working against the famine. In response to her appeal, in November that year, Pope Benedict XV wrote the encyclical letter entitled *Paterno Iam Diu,* in which he beseeched all churches

---

[31] http://www.savethechildren.it/chi_siamo/storia.html.

of the world to collect funds for children. In 1920, in the further encyclical *Annus iam Planus est* he openly praised *Save the Children* for its work. It was the first time in history that the Catholic Church supported a cause promoted by a non-confessional organization[32].

In 1921, Save the Children helped Russian children struck by famine. Today, the organization is the largest independent association for the protection and promotion of children's rights. It is operational in over 100 countries, and gives aid to families and children in emergencies, whether due to natural disasters or war. It enjoys consultative status at the Economic and Social Council of the United Nations. It speaks in the name of children and lobbies governments and national and international institutions. During World War I, Eglantyne was struck by the suffering that war inflicted on children; persuaded as she was that "wars are always, first and foremost, wars against children", she deemed it necessary to affirm some fundamental rights for children specifically.

"It appears that the time has come when it is no longer possible to wait for the establishment of broad-ranging welfare plans" she wrote to her sister Suzanne. *"If, despite everything, we wish to continue to work for children . . . it appears that the only way possible is to invoke a joint effort by nations to protect their children in constructive, rather than charitable, ways. I believe that we should vindicate the fundamental rights of children and work for their recognition throughout the world."*

"It was March 1922 when Eglantyne first proposed that Save the Children adopt a document "defining the duties of adults towards children, which each country should recognise either by means of State intervention or by private action". A few months later she circulated a draft of her "Children's Charter" to the British Save

---

[32]   "[…] Nor will we ever cease praising the goodness of God, who loved that such Christian charity could by our means be showered on our little abandoned children. To this end, we cannot omit to give public praise to the society called *"Save the Children Fund"*, because it spared no care or diligence to collect funds, clothing and food" Encyclical letter *Annus Iam Plenus (1920)* of Pope Benedict XV to the Patriarchs, Primates, Archbishops, Bishops and other local ordained in peace and communion with the apostolic see: that the children of the wealthier countries contribute to alleviating the suffering of those who have nothing.

the Children for comments and that autumn she started work on three separate papers: a declaration of rights, a legislative code to be embodied in a future Convention of Geneva and an outline of work to be done by both the State and private organizations. The actual declaration of rights was to be "general and fundamental and such as to command universal assent", Eglantyne wrote. "They are in the nature of principles. They should be sound, indisputable and universally valid".

But Eglantyne's was not the only children's charter under discussion in 1922. The International Council for Women was developing a detailed document with seven categories marshalling fifty-one clauses into order, "based on the principle that every child is born with the inalienable right to have the opportunity of full physical, mental and spiritual development . . ." Lady Aberdeen, the President of the International Council for Women, was also a member of the British Save the Children Fund and it was soon suggested that this charter should inform or even replace, the briefer Save the Children document of which Lady Aberdeen disapproved. By January 1923 Eglantyne's proposed "Children Charter: A declaration of the rights of Childhood" had been fundamentally compromised. The "declaration of Rights" subtitle had been dropped, the fifteen clauses extended to twenty-eight and tangled up in welfare details and the opening phrase of each clause: "It is the right of every child . . ." had been changed to "every child should . . ." as in "should be brought up, as much as possible, in the open air and sunshine". In effect it was no longer a bold statement of children's rights, but a rather woolly list of the reponsibilities of governments towards children; a not-so-subtle shift that made the child the recipient of state protection rather than the bearer of rights and responsibilities appropriate to his or her age.

Eglantyne was hugely critical of the Women's Council charter for "summing up the duties of the state towards children", while at the same time being "to my mind too socialistic". "At present however" she now furiously told Suzanne in a series of letters written in both pen and penci, whichever came to hand first," I prefer Lady Aberdeen's charter to ours, for the SCF council has cut out all its more important provisions, retaining the questions of details which are puerile without the others". "The Charter I drafted originally has been entirely spoilt" she was still going two days later, "the result is ludicrous".

Somewhat tactlessly and naively in January 1923 the British Save the Children council proposed that Eglantyne take the revised Children's Charter to the February meeting of the Save the Children International Union in Geneva for approval. Eglantyne had other ideas: "I am hoping the Union will turn it down!!"" she confessed to Suzanne.

With the support of Etienne Clouzot, The Union's General Secretary who had been her close ally since the days in 1920 when they were both involved in setting up the international organization, she quickly revised her own brief statement, translated it into what she called her "execrable French" and pressed for it to be adopted. Months of painful consultation and revisions followed with more than one vote for a clause to cover the child before birth which was ultimately rejected on the grounds that it would reduce the unity and simplicity of the document. Finally the "Declaration of the Rights of the Child" was adopted by the International Union on 17 May 1923.

THE DECLARATION OF THE RIGHTS OF THE CHILD (1923)

By the present Declaration of the Rights of the Child, commonly known as the "Declaration of Geneva" men and women of all nations recognizing that Mankind owes to the Child the best it has to give declare and accept it as their duty that beyond and above all considerations of race, nationality or creed:

I   THE CHILD must be given the means requisite for its normal development, both materially and spiritually.
II THE CHILD that is hungry must be fed; the child that is sick must be nursed; the child that is backward must be helped; the delinquent child must be reclaimed; and the orphan and waif must be sheltered and succoured.
III THE CHILD must be the first to receive relief in times of distress.
IV THE CHILD must be in position to earn a livelihood and must be protected against every form of exploitation.
V   THE CHILD must be brought up in the consciousness that its talents must be devoted to the service of its fellow-men.

Four of these five points focus on the child's rights to protection and provision based on Save the Children's experience in international relief and development. Eglantyne had no concept that children's rights might later be discussed in terms of empowerment or the right to degrees of self-determination but protection has remained the enduring basis of children's legal rights. However she was very aware of the problems involved in trying to reconcile individual and cultural differences in a statement of the universal. "Everything should be done to avoid imposing a uniform type of culture . . ." she wrote with impressive vision; "The methods of child nurture must necessarily vary greatly according to differences of climate, race, traditions, beliefs, etc. But nevertheless there are certain fundamental principles which should be respected however much the means of their practical application may differ in different localities".

Eglantyne's last, rather innovative interpretation of what a right entails that the child "be brought up in the consciousness that its talents must be devoted to the service of its fellowmen" was clearly the product of her own climate, reflecting the importance she attached to New Liberal ideas around citizenship and the twinning of rights with responsibilities. Eglantyne's focus here was not with the immediate needs and rights of children as children but with the child as future citizen; the symbolic child that represented the next generation. The future of the world is with the child" she scribbled on the top of an early draft.

At the First Assembly of the League, Gustave Ador of the Swiss delegation, The International Red Cross and the Save the Children International Union brought a resolution in support of agencies working "on behalf of children affected by war" and proposing a High Commissioner for Children be appointed to co-ordinate the relief work already being undertaken. Although the General Assembly got excited about the role, optimistically recording that "these millions of children rescued from death and deprivation will remember when they become men the debt they have contracted towards the League of Nations when it (was) just beginning", in fact the idea of a Children's Commissioner soon fell off the agenda. It was not until June 1921 when a joint letter from the Red Cross and Save the Children asking the Council of the League for a section dedicated to the protection of children led to the formation of an independent bureau, reflecting the growing sympathy towards the child as an instrument of peace. "Henceforth the children of the world will be under the protection of the League of Nations" the English press reported. After several different incarnations this bureau became the League of Nations Child Welfare Committee in 1924. Eglantyne was appointed an assessor.

One of her first contributions was to propose that "the League of Nations should recognize the question of the protection of children as one of its fundamental duties . . ." on the rather Victorian premise that "every child whose normal physical, intellectual or moral development is hindered is a potential source of disorder and a danger to the community". After a silence so tangible it can almost be heard in the minutes, the next point raised proposed that "the Committee should confine itself to resolutions dealing with definite points to be discussed". Even so, being composed of an eclectic collection of "experts" commenting on a shared agenda, it inevitably took the Committee a while to become effective.

Before long however Eglantyne was making valuable and sometimes quite uncomfortable contributions such as pointing out that of the twenty-two members of the committee, which was meant to offer global representation, eighteen were European and of those six were English. Only two members represented the Americas and one Asia. Africa had no representation.

As a result many of the issues under discussion such as family allowances or "the effect of cinema on the mental and moral wellbeing of children" were of little or no relevance to children in the majority of the world.

Eglantyne herself only submitted reports when she felt the subject was of international relevance such as a sixty-four-page memo on "the assistance or repatriation of foreign children who are abandoned, neglected or delinquent" which stressed that children should be considered within the context of their families and communities, and given assistance within their own country wherever possible; policy that was later reflected in the relevant convention and is still considered best practice today. After thanking the committee for their positive response to her report, she commented rather dryly that "judging by the number of conventions in existence, it might be imagined that the problem had been solved; but this was not the cause". It was later agreed to limit the field of investigation to such international issues to avoid invading the domestic policy of member states as well as over-whelming the committee.

On this basis Eglantyne and Suzanne presented a report on the constructive work of the Union around the protection and welfare of children which was well received and Eglantyne supported a range of proposals from the central collection of reliable information for use by voluntary associations, to the banning of children under fourteen from employment. Often the work led to new conventions not all of which were well received. "We would not sign your resolution because child refugees are not a problem here" the British government responded with ill-concealed irritation to one proposal "it would therefore only create unnecessary admin . . .".

Eglantyne's main agenda while at the League, however, was to promote the Declaration of the Rights of the Child. It now became evident she had been wise to keep the document short: "the more deeply a convention goes into a question", one footnote to discussions ran, "the less likely it is to be concluded". Even so at first there was some ambivalence towards the declaration and its authors within the League; once the emergency work of the famine became less pressing there was feeling that the Save the Children International Union had lost its focus. But with the support of Charlie and the British delegation, the declaration was finally brought before the Assembly on a wet September day in 1924.

Eglantyne did not have the authority to address the Assembly herself but on 26 September Giuseppe Motta, President of the Assembly of the League and a former Swiss President, supported by the Labour Prime Minister Ramsay Mac Donald, brought the declaration before the League's Fifth Commission, dealing with child welfare. A motion of approval, chaired by Valdes Mendeville, the candidate from Chile, was carried unanimously. "The Assembly endorses the declaration of the rights of the child, commonly known as the Declaration of Geneva", the minutes record "and invites the State Members of the League to be guided by its principles in the work of child welfare". In an idiosyncratic act of thanksgiving Eglantyne arranged for a service of dedication at St Martin in the Fields in Trafalgar Square at which representatives of the Church of England, Free Churches, Orthodox and Armenian Churches all took part.

The next job was advocacy. At a conference called by the Save the Children International Union in both Vienna and Budapest a month after the declaration had been endorsed by the League, Eglantyne called on participating nations to adopt their own children's charters against which to regularly assess the situation of their country's children. Information cards given out had the Declaration printed in full on the reverse and it was quickly reproduced in national papers across Europe. Germany, Belgium, Sweden and Canada all used it as the basis to form national laws for child welfare.

Other signatories over the next year included King Boris of Bulgaria, Frau Marianne Hainisch, mother of the first President of Austria and Prime Ministers of Britain, Australia, South Africa, New Zealand, Canada and Newfoundland then a separate territory.

In the Republic of Ireland the declaration was the only document to be signed by both the President of the Irish Free State and the Republican leader, Eamon de Valera.

In France the Minister for Public Instruction ordered a copy to be hung in every school. Eglantyne, who had always wanted the declaration to be actively supported by everyone in contact with children not just government departments making policy was delighted by this last idea. She quickly organized a children's drawing competition among schools in fourteen exhibited countries to illustrate the declaration's clauses. Two thousand entries were exhibited internationally, generating huge press coverage and public interest.

The following year, 1925, the Union organized the first "General Congress on Child Welfare". Seven hundred delegates attended this seminal event in Geneva, including the representatives of thirty-eight governments and fifty-four nations. If their diverse interests presented certain problems, from Eglantyne's perspective it meant that the event was "rich also in possibilities of which you had scarcely dreamed". Above all, she felt that the discussion, structured around the clauses of the declaration, highlighted the need to "universalize the work which is being done in small patches here and there" and set the scene for a new "concerted effort". "Sometimes you feel you turn a corner and pass through a door" she concluded: "Is it too much to hope that it may mark our entrance into a new era when the Declaration will be made the charter of a new civilization?".

A new civilization is ambitious but this is a new era for children's rights. Eglantyne's simple declaration has now evolved into the "united Nations Convention on the Rights of the Child" which, ratified by all but two countries around the world is the most universally accepted human rights instrument in history, making children a central concern of the global community. In encoding children's rights into international law the Convention provides agreed standards against which a country's progress can be both organized and independently assessed and makes governments legally accountable for failing to meet the needs of children.

However, the most serious criticism is that if children's rights are now recognized, arguably they remain on the international agenda because of the world's failure to meet its obligations under the convention. Somalia, which does not have a fully recognized government, and the USA, which wants to retain its legal rights both to execute children under eighteen and put them in the front line of battle, are both yet to ratify the convention. And, perhaps worse, many ratifying governments have failed to develop a coherent strategy or allocate sufficient resources to implement the convention. All over the world children are neglected and abused, forced to become soldiers or work long hours, detained in immigration centers, denied healthcare, education and even the playtime simply to be children. The principle of "all children, all rights" is still much too far from being a reality", the former UN Secretary General Kofi Annan has admitted and Save the Children has reported that "millions of lives . . . have been barely touched by the UNCRC".

But if not the complete solution, the convention has had powerful impact for many millions of children around the world. Eglantyne's declaration for the first time enshrined the moral equality of children with adults and its endorsement by the League of Nations put children's rights, as distinct within broader human rights discourse, firmly on the international legal map. The convention now provides the impetus for governments to make a reality of children's rights through consultation, legal protection and the provision of welfare services, with independent agencies like Save the Children, UNICEF and national children's ombudsmen able to hold those governments to account.

It is perhaps too hopeful to imagine a world with no neglect or abuse of children, the utopian "new civilization" that Eglantyne had hoped for. But the promotion of children's rights has structured the work not only of governments and development organizations but all the social institutions that impact on children's lives from schools and medical practices to courts and detention centers around the world. The modern perception of child welfare being a right rather than a privilege and the increasingly active climate of consideration of children would have pleased Eglantyne, who recognized that any declaration or convention only becomes valuable when applied and that real progress in making a reality of children's rights lies in a new respect between children and adults being reflected not only in conventions and laws but also in social institutions, practices and attitudes. "It is not much use in passing laws unless the whole community are endeavoring to carry out the principle underlying them, "she wrote to Suzanne in 1923. "Everybody . . . everyone who in any way comes into contact with children—that is to say the vast majority of mankind—may be in a position to help". Eglantyne put children's rights on the world's agenda; the responsibility for upholding them now lies with us"[33].

Eglantyne died in Geneva in 1928, only 52 years old. With her personal courage, charisma and human vision, she had won over much of the aristocracy and trade unions, the Pope and the Bolshevik government, the wife of the Prime Minister who had organized the economic bloc, and the newborn League of Nations in Geneva.

"To be successful in life, it is necessary to give life". She did not do so by becoming a mother, as would have been expected of a wealthy woman of Edwardian times, but through the creation of the Save the Children Fund.

Although her story has been mostly forgotten, and children's rights have yet to be fully achieved, Eglantyne's success in drawing to them the attention of the world's political agenda attests to the strength of her humanitarian spirit. Eglantyne Jebb personally found children noisy and tiring, and even went so far as calling them "pests", but saw the future in them. She sensed that failing to protect and respect children is a risk and danger for society.

---

[33] Mulley, at note 1, pp. 305-316.

CHAPTER 7

LIDIA POET

(Traverse, 1855-Diano Marina 1949)
The lawyer who could not practice

Law is one of the professions that has most tenaciously resisted granting access to women.

Latin historians provide some examples of female patrons. Valerius Maximus cites Caia Afrania, who caused a scandal after a praetorial edict banned women from postulating for others but not for themselves; he also tells us of a certain Mesia (perhaps Amesia Sentia) who defended herself against accused crimes, and was later absolved and declared "androgynous", since "*sub specie foeminae virile animum gerebat*" [under a female appearance, she carried a male soul].

Roman women were sometimes also allowed to deal with cases that were not wholly personal. For example, Hortensia, the daughter of the orator Hortensius, "consistently and happily" took on a case to defend the "*ordo matronarum*", upon which taxes had been imposed, since it had not been possible to find any male defender.

Indeed, while professions such as teaching or medicine had opened to women, albeit in restricted fields such as nurseries and specializations in pediatrics, because women were recognized as having particular maternal and social skills, the legal professions required political and public skills that were usually not associated with female nature.

Lidia Poet[34] was a brilliant student, and graduated in law on 17 June 1881 from the University of Turin. Her dissertation was on the role of women in society, and she dedicated it to her mother and her brother Enrico, both of whom had guided and supported her, in words and by example.

The dissertation was a thorough essay on feminism, discussing its historical roots and focusing especially on the issue of women's right to vote, which was hotly debated in those years, especially pursuant to the English suffragettes' violent actions.

"After graduating, Lidia Poet asked to be admitted to the register of legal practitioners (25 July 1881) and performed the requisite two years of training at Pinerolo. She took and passed the exams required by law to become prosecutor, pursuant to which she asked to be enrolled in the official Registry of Lawyers.

Poet's request provoked great surprise in Turin's legal circles and gave rise to volatile debates, as hers was the first such case in the entire Kingdom of Italy.

The Council of the Turin Bar Association examined the issue on 1 August 1883, [. . .] when it met to decide Poet's request. As prescribed by law, Poet had performed her training at a law firm, attended the required hearings, passed the exam and had a clean criminal record.

She was therefore fully qualified to have her request approved[35].

Some of the Bar's lawyers and advisers were against her admission, as the law had not taken women into consideration: it was absurd and improper for women, whether married or not, to appear in tribunals and courtrooms; furthermore, once she was admitted, she could even aspire to becoming a judge.

---

[34] In her book *La toga negata* (Alzani, Pinerolo, 1997), Clara Bounous consulted the archives of the Municipality and Waldensian Church of Perrero, as well as several texts at the National Library of Turin and the judgments of the Courts of Appeal and Cassation of Turin at the state Archives. Some relatives of Lidia Poet were also contacted, to gain a full picture of her personal and professional profile.

[35] The quotes that follow are taken from the files for 1881 at the Bar Association of Turin.

[. . .] No law had ever purported to remove women from the ordinary household occupations proper to them [. . .]. It was never sought to "place them in greater sight than necessary, educated and intelligent as they may be".

However, the President of the Council and other advisers disagreed. They specified that "according to Italian civil legislation, women are citizens, just like men". They therefore enjoyed all civil rights, with limited exceptions, and it would have been outdated to keep to the old path, because the legal trends of the times all tended towards equality.

Thus, the majority of the Council did not deny Lidia Poet's admission, since she had fulfilled all prerequisites[36].

This decision gave rise to much controversy and debate: some of the Bar Association's advisers resigned in protest, as they saw Poet's admission as an act of contempt towards the prestige and traditions of the Association itself[37].

Those who were against admitting women to the Bar advanced further arguments in their support.

First, it was certain that the legislator had intended to exclude women from the legal profession. According to Article 1743 of the Civil Code, women could not accept mandates without their husband's authorization; therefore, a woman who did not have her husband's consent would not have been able to "draft donation contracts, take care of sales of land, verify membership statuses and arrange mortgages, draft contracts for loans, defend others in court. [. . .] She would be a lawyer [. . .] who, for the performance of many of her functions, would depend on a family meeting [. . .], a lawyer who would be subjected to a multiplicity of limitations which would be essentially contrary to the nature and practical performance of the profession"[38].

The law imposed restrictions upon unmarried women too. It was therefore impossible for women who were not granted the

---

[36] Bounous, at note 1, pp. 53-54.

[37] C. F. Gabba, *Le donne non avvocate*, Pisa, 1884.

[38] A. Bianchi, *Sull'esercizio delle professioni di avvocato e procuratore*, Casa editrice, Torino, 1885, pp. 124-125.

guardianship of a minor, or of legally incompetent individuals, to be recognized as lawyers.

The Appeal

"The Turin Bar's courageous decision did not close the thorny issue, as the King's General Prosecutor of the Court of Appeal of Turin strongly opposed Poet's admission. Lidia thus lodged two counterclaims.

On 6 September 1883, Prosecutor General Giuseppe Magenta challenged the case. For women, "the title of lawyer and practice of law is not admissible, for the sole but essential reason that the title and practice cannot, by law, be taken by women".

While it was broadly possible to speak of legal and political equality between the sexes, stated the Prosecutor, this was not so considering the aptitudes, the inclinations that led women to remain within the family.

Lidia Poet's answer was resolute and firm: these claims were more rhetorical than legal, inspired by feelings. To affirm that "the aptitudes, the inclinations, the mission that are supposedly proper to women are irreconcilable with the practice of law, that her intellect be insufficiently strong, her knowledge not of the desired breadth, her labor not be tireless, might be the opinion of the learned General Prosecutor and of several other respectable figures, an opinion that perhaps, time and facts will change."

Furthermore, the opinion that the legal profession would have distracted women from their natural domestic occupations to the detriment of the family was entirely unfounded, as the duties were absolutely not incompatible. Many women who were teachers, female doctors, engineers or professors, and even factory workers, already worked outside the home, and they had not been denied the opportunity to work.

Some weeks later, the General Prosecutor presented a new claim. The arguments were not new: the law of 1874 did not abolish the exclusion of women from free exercise of the legal profession, and a law degree was merely a certificate of scientific knowledge.

He thus declared his opposition to the decision taken by the Council of the Turin Bar, which should not have admitted Lidia Poet.

Poet once again answered with a long dissertation, in which she reiterated that the law of 1874 did not exclude women from the legal profession; if it were otherwise, it would have contained express provisions to that effect.

The Court of Appeal examined the claims and counterclaims. It upheld the Prosecutor's claims on the basis of the legislation currently in force; it held that the law did not give women the possibility of practicing law[39].

The judgment stated that "today, moreover, it would be improper and ugly to see women descend into the court's gymnasium, excite themselves among the noise of public judgment, participate heatedly in discussions that easily reach excess, and in which, in spite of themselves, they may be drawn beyond the limits that the fairest sex ought to observe [. . .]. There is no need to mention the risk to the soundness of judgments, should one see the judicial robe or the lawyer's headgear worn over the strange and bizarre clothing which fashion often imposes on women, and no less bizarre hairdos"[40].

The case before the Court of Cassation

"After the Court of Appeal's decision, Lidia Poet played her last card: on 28 November 1883, she lodged an appeal with the Turin Court of Cassation, arguing that the grounds alleged against her admission to the Bar constituted violations and erroneous applications of legislation.

According to the first argument, women were excluded from the legal profession because there was no law enabling them to access it. Poet conceded that there was no such law, but highlighted that there was also no law that excluded her.

The second opposition was based on the absence of a legal provision that allowed women to exercise a public and civil office. Poet objected that the legal profession was not a public office, but a

---

[39] From the judgment handed down on 11 November 1883 by the Turin Court of Appeal, Turin State Archives.

[40] *Ibid.*

private profession that is pursued for remuneration or for leisure, as expressly stated in the Law of 1874.

However, her appeal was in vain: on 18 April 1884, the Court of Cassation upheld the judgment of the Court of Appeal.

In its judgment, the Court first lavished praise on Poet, who "had applied herself to practical studies with fervent effort and intelligent laboriousness, demonstrating and deploying a singular and distinguished aptitude, as honorable witnesses have said of her [. . .]; with this same diligence she attended the hearings of the Tribunals [. . .], and passed the theoretical-practical exam". Lidia Poet was also "a remarkable example of firm purpose of strength of will and perseverant industriousness, and aptitude for elevated and difficult studies".

The Court then reprised the usual reasoning, maintaining that it was necessary to consider the special mission conferred upon women by their nature, to which sensitive and vital social interests were tied. If Italian women had achieved many civil rights not previously enjoyed, and could engage in many public activities, professions and function, the Court nevertheless thought it necessary to recall that perfecting the law was a task of the legislator, and not of the judge, as the latter only had the task of interpreting and applying the legislation in force."[41]

After this judgment, Lidia Poet dropped the case but continued to work for society.

The debate in Parliament

The Poet case generated much controversy. Books, articles, dissertations of all sorts were published and sparked a debate that reached the Parliament.

Thus, the issue passed to the political class, but ultimately remained unchanged.

"During the Chamber of Deputies' session of June 2nd, 1884, after having asked in vain the Keeper of the Seals whether provisions were being made to ensure the full application of the 1874 law on the legal profession, the *onorevole* [Member of Parliament] Bertani again questioned the legal issues of the problem.

---

[41] Bounous, at note 1, pp. 67-69.

The latter believed that the law did not exclude women from the legal profession. As a doctor, he reminded the audience of how male doctors did not prevent women's entry into their profession"[42].

The subject was reprised by the Senate, and in particular Senator Moleschott, on June 28th. He disagreed with the Turin judgment and asked the floor whether it was to be considered irrevocable. The senator did not declare himself a fanatic of women's emancipation, as he considered women to be principally "the educator of their children, of brothers, of sisters, a moderator, an advisor to her husband and her friends [. . .] as one who cheers life with the sweetest affections; tempers the ardor and enlivens the courage of men; and in the great struggles of life, as in the great sorrows, it is she alone who has been worthy of deserving the image of the consoling angel". However, he also did not wish to impede women's path, if they are moved by a heartfelt vocation[43].

In concrete terms, the debate was fruitless. The issue was forgotten for many years.

Lidia Poet had been defeated on the legal level, but did not encounter any obstacles to her social initiatives and and generosity.

In 1890 she traveled to St. Petersburg to expound her ideas on the theoretical and practical problems of prisons.

Poet believed that four objectives had to be achieved: giving further dignity to penal studies as a specific branch of criminal law or as an independent subject to be studied from secondary school; the promotion of public conferences for the educated classes; the importation, from the United States, the institution of "prisoner Sundays" once or twice a year to educate the people on what is being done, or is sought to be done, to repress and morally elevate prisoners; and finally, the promotion of the publication and circulation of books, textbooks and studies on the subject"[44].

Poet represented Italy at the Congress of Rome of May 1914. Her contribution concerned the moral and legal assistance to be given to minors.

---

[42]   E. Ollandini, *La donna e l'avvocatura. Studio storico-giuridico-sociale*, Genoa, 1913, p. 255.

[43]   *Ibid.*, p. 267.

[44]   Bounous, at 1, pp. 71-74.

She maintained that, as the authority of the family as a social institution was progressively declining, the education of children was a crucial problem, one upon which all others depended, as youth would be the society of the future.

For these reasons, it was necessary to lay grounds favorable to the education of minors: in the past, this was done by the father of the family; now it was time to involve schools and the society, which however were often not up to the job. The fast-paced lifestyle of the period took much away from fathers and mothers; this was especially true in working-class families, where the work schedule prevented parents from taking care of their children's interior lives. Especially in big cities, children were abandoned to themselves, susceptible to undesirable encounters and events and thus moral degeneration.

Poet proposed a project to reform juvenile detention which in Italy was certainly ahead of its times. It can be summarized with a slogan, formulated in 1885 in the occasion of another Congress: "For abandoned children, build less prisons and more reformatories, less reformatories and more houses of education".

The extraordinary modernity of her ideas lies in grasping that a criminal is not recuperated through repression but rather through education, if he has not received any education—by teaching him orderliness and a healthy lifestyle, and tending a hand so that he no longer engages in crime.

These topics remain debated and at least party unresolved to this day. For them, Lidia Poet fought stubbornly on civil and legal fronts for much of her life. She traveled throughout Europe and lived a life of extraordinary social activism.

She became part of the Secretariat of the International Prison Conference and represented Italy in several parts of the world, as Vice-President of the Legal Department.

She was personally involved in issues relating to penology, prisons and prisoners, always impassioned and tireless.

The French Government appointed her *Officier d'Academie*. In Paris she met Venizelos, the Cretan hero, who told her: "I have always been against women who want to do a man's job, but seeing you, I change my mind". At the beginning of the war, Lidia Poet became a volunteer for the Red Cross. She applied herself to her new mission with such intensity that her health suffered; for her work of aid to soldiers and civilians injured in the war, she received a silver medal.

In a speech before the Chamber of Deputies on April 16th, 1918, *onorevole* Orlando confessed his opposition in principle to granting women the vote, but considered that the times had changed; the war had revealed the social importance of female work, and it was therefore necessary to acknowledge this in some way.

From 1906, the troubled journey of women's access to the Bar received precious help from the courageous judge, lawyer and professor Ludovico Mortara, who was also a Minister and Keeper of the Seals. World War I was a pivotal moment, as it opened more jobs to women. In 1919, thanks to Mortara, the institution of marital authorization was abolished, which cleared this obstacle to women's admission to the Bar. Law No. 1126 of 9 March 1919 was approved; this allowed women, on an equal basis to men, to practice the professions and all public positions except those which required the exercise of jurisdictional public powers, the exercise of rights and political authority or that concerned the military defense of the State.

So, the claims advanced by Lidia Poet and a few other women who continued her fight, such as the Roman lawyer Teresa Labriol, had finally been accepted, after almost forty years of struggle. For Lidia Poet, admission to the Bar came too late, as she was already sixty-four, but she still asked to be admitted to the Turin Bar, on November 20, 1920.

Italy thus took a step forward, in the same direction as other countries already had, although women's right to vote and to access the judicial profession were yet to be recognized (respectively, 1946 and 1963)[45].

Lidia Poet was of a wealthy family, but did not marry nor have children. She died on 25 February 1949 in Diano Marina, fully lucid and still able to read and write without glasses.

The local newspapers reported the news: "Lawyer Lidia Poet, born in Traverse and a member of the Church of Pinerolo, died in Diano Marina at the age of 94 years old, in the serenity of an old age enlightened by faith, after a life devoted to noble ideals of good,

---

[45] The Unitd States in 1856, Sweden in 1897, Switzerland in 1899, France in 1900, Norway in 1904, Denmark in 1906, England in 1919, Austria in 1920 (German and Belgium only in 1922).

which in her were the precious fruit of a Christian inspiration of life. During her funerary mass celebrated in Pinerolo, as the coffin traveled towards the cemetery of San Martino (Perrero), lawyer Mario Risso, with lofty words, wished to commemorate the life and work of the lawyer Lidia Poet and to offer to her memory the commendation of the Board of Lawyers".

The Turin Bar wrote: "With reverent regret the Bar remembers its lawyer Lidia Poet, renowned interpreter of the vindication of women in the professional mission and in legal and social reforms".

On her tombstone, at the cemetery of San Martino, the following inscription is sculpted: "First female lawyer of Italy lived in God. To her family, to her friends in need she bestowed goods, time, works. The heartfelt regret of her loved ones follows her"[46].

---

[46]   Bounous, at note 1, pp. 103-104.

Chapter 8

LINA FURLAN

(Venice, 8 September 1903-Turin, 26 August 2000)
The first practicing female lawyer

"Having acquired spiritual enlightenment, I met a woman who was to continue leading me in the world of spirituality. Contrary to what one may suppose, this woman is not a creature haloed in mystery, adorned with indecipherable symbols, who walks barefoot on the dewy asphodels of an impossible world. She is an achieving woman. She is the wise woman of the Sacred Scriptures. She showed me that the strength of the spirit can change the course of human destiny.

This woman practices a masculine profession. She is a lawyer. [. . .] She tears not from justice, but from injustice, her preys, through the exquisite resources of her female mind.

Her name is Lina Furlan and she is Italian by birth, traditions, sensitivity. She was born in Venice, the Adriatic city of the Doges, where another great female lawyer, Portia of Shakespeare's Merchant of Venice, defended the weak against the powerful. [. . .]"
(Pitigrilli on Pitigrilli, Sonzogno, Milan, 1949, pp. 231-237)

Lina Furlan's story follows Lidia Poet's troubled efforts to enable women's access to the legal profession fifty years before any female presence in the courtrooms was admitted.

"Turin was once again to be the setting of an important event during the Fascist era: on October 30th, 1929, for the first time, an Italian woman delivered a speech before the Court of Assizes, thus launching a new course for the legal profession and vindicating the right enshrined in Law No. 1976 of 1919"[47].

Lina Furlan was born in Venice in 1903, and went to Turin to follow her brother, who had been called to FIAT, the great Italian car producer, by its President Giovanni Agnelli.

She studied law first in Bologna and then in Turin, and in the meantime also attended the Dresden *Hochschule* to learn German, literature and art history.

After graduating in 1926, she passed the exams to become a lawyer in 1929 and began to practice.

In her first case, she successfully defended a young female factory worker who had committed infanticide, but had been a victim of her brutally violent father.

Lidia Poet had attended the trial, and at the end embraced her colleague, moved to tears.

Furlan always sought to present the human side of her clients, especially women; she never banged her fists on the table, unlike her colleagues; she did not raise her voice in the courtroom; she did not seek at all costs to be the protagonist, but rather to capture her clients' humanity.

In the early stages of her career, Furlan was often asked why she was in the courtroom; unperturbed, she would reply that the 1919 law had opened the legal profession to women too.

At first, her clients were only men, but eventually included women too. Furlan often acted on a *pro bono* basis to help those who could not pay for their legal representatives.

In 1938 she met Pitigrilli, a pseudonym of Dino Segre, a controversial figure who later became her husband.

Segre was a writer and a journalist who had been tasked to write an article on Lina for the periodical "*Grandi Firme*", since she was one of the few women to affirm herself in the legal profession.

The two met, and married in 1940. However, their union had to be kept secret as Pitigrilli was Jewish; indeed, they hid their relationship for a long time.

World War II was an extremely trying period for both: Segre was sent to L'Aquila, their house was ransacked and then confiscated,

---

[47]   Clara Bounous, *La toga negata*, Alzani, Pinerolo, Turin 1197, p. 95.

and in 1943 Furlan was forced to flee to Switzerland with their six-month-old son. She then traveled to Paris and South America (Brazil, Argentina, Peru).

Once she returned to Italy, Lina Furlan again applied for admission to the Turin Bar. From that moment, she never stopped working.

Her courtroom work sought to prove and persuade, without grandeur but with firmness. People said that she had a dual personality which combined faith and elegance, worldliness and reserve, a fighting spirit and mercy.

Some of the cases argued during her youth highlight her nature as a steadfast and sensible Catholic woman, as well as her uncompromising behavior in the courtroom.

"In the first trial, she defended a priest who had defected during the war—a very serious crime for those times. The priest had asked to take part in the war as a chaplain, to assist the dying and to celebrate the Holy Mass, or as a nurse in a field hospital. Instead, due to an administrative mistake, he was assigned to an infantry unit. He did not want to kill as he was a priest of Christ, who had taught man to love his enemies. However, there could be no justifications in the eyes of the Military Tribunal, which applied a rigid and uncompromising Code. The Attorney General had asked for the highest penalty to be imposed upon the priest, to set an example.

In court, Lina Furlan spoke for one hour, leaving aside the law and the Penal Code to invoke only the laws of Christian love. In one hand she held the Code, and in the other, the Gospel. She spoke of God, who cautions men who judge and are judged.

For a moment, the figures of authority in the courtroom appeared to shed their distinguished uniforms and to return being simple men. The two policemen who held the defendant could not stop their tears. The President of the Court embarrassedly exclaimed "It is not possible to discuss a case in this atmosphere. Furlan, I call you to order!"[48]

Finally, Mussolini ordered that the trial be suspended and resumed at the end of the war, and that the priest be returned to the front as a chaplain. The priest died there, as he wished, while carrying an injured man on his shoulders.

---

[48] Cfr. *Pitigrilli parla di Pitigrilli*, Sonzogno, Milan, 1949.

In the second case, Lina Furlan defended a mother who had allegedly been an accomplice to a murder committed by her husband. The problem was that the key witness was a 7-year-old child, excluded from the courtroom by law. Furlan had him admitted anyway amidst general disapproval; to the objections raised by the President of the Court, she answered "certainly, but children cannot be abandoned on the streets. The child is in the care of an aunt, who is a witness in the present trial, and would therefore be alone today. He will not be seated in the public gallery, he will be here among the lawyers and I will keep him close to my place"[49].

The President acquiesced and instructed the lawyers to abstain from questioning the child; he ordered the boy to sit in the place of the prosecution lawyers, far from the defense.

His father had killed a man and buried him in the forest, while his mother was accused of being her husband's accomplice.

After several witnesses' depositions, the Public Prosecutor's summing up and his father's defense, a certain storm was mentioned.

The child suddenly looked at his mother and cried "No, on the day that it rained, Mother stayed at home all day, next to me, because we were sick. I was crying".

The little boy had spoken words of truth which remained sculpted in the judges' hearts. The prosecution was disarmed and Lina Furlan no longer needed the child to testify; the woman was released for lack of proof. A colleague asked Lina what she had prompted the child to say. She answered "I told him nothing; who spoke to him was God"[50].

From this answer emerges a woman who possessed entrenched moral principles permeated with modernity, a woman who knows her limits and tries for a surprise effect, but, especially, who has also has unshakeable faith in the supreme God.

Indeed, Lina was a devout Catholic and had even met some Popes, among whom Pius XII, Paul VI and John XXIII.

Her female sensitivity and Catholic upbringing were clear especially in her defense of maternity, which she believed was was the greatest privilege women had over men"[51].

---

[49] Pitigrilli, *cit.*

[50] Pitigrilli, *cit.*

[51] Bounous, *op. cit.*, pp. 99-101.

Lina was happy with what life had given her: "I would practice law again, but in another form. I would trust others less. I have spread my arms beyond what I was capable of embracing. Today, I would defend myself more from the world, from turpitude.

To a young woman, I would say 'Go, in all earnestness, be ready to work less intensely if you become a mother; thank God for defending yourself, be your own watch and try not to be overwhelmed'.[52]"

---

[52] *Ibid.*, pp. 103-104.

CHAPTER 9

ELEANOR ROOSEVELT

(New York, 11 October 1884-New York, 7 November 1962)
A rhino's hide

"Hate and force cannot be in just a part of the world without having an effect on the rest of it."

"It isn't enough to talk about peace. One must believe in it. And it isn't enough to believe in it. One must work at it."

"All too often, important decisions are born and have taken shape in entities consisting entirely of men, or at least so entirely dominated by them that any contribution of very special value that women may offer is cast aside, without comment".

"From the ruins of World War II, a small group of authoritative historians, philosophers, diplomats and jurists, all from different cultures—Catholic, Protestant, Islamic, Jewish, Confucian, atheist, Hindu—, thanks to the intelligent, impassioned and tenacious guidance of Eleanor Roosevelt, managed to glean the common values at the foundation of a peaceful human consortium, and collected them in that document that can be defined as the first Bill of Rights of all humanity: the Universal Declaration of Human Rights of 1948. Eleanor Roosevelt's human sensitivity and tenaciousness made a decisive contribution to the patient weaving of the threads of human and cultural relations upon which the Declaration is based.

All the processes that led to the approval of the constitutional texts after World War II overcame the deep ideological and political divisions of those who had been summoned to the negotiation table.

The Declaration too originates from the meeting of a group of persons—Charles Malik, Peng-chun Chang, René Cassin, John P. Humphrey, Hansa Mehta and Roosevelt herself—a meeting which mysteriously made possible that which, on paper, seemed impossible. It was not only a skilled work of synthesis between different cultural traditions—Oriental, Arab, Western—, or between different world visions—liberal, Catholic, socialist—, but of a meeting of persons who expressed various cultures yet could not fail to recognize themselves in a common humanity"[53].

Many of the group's members had enthusiastically read or heard the speech on the "four freedoms" delivered by Franklin Roosevelt in 1941, in which he said that future peace and security depended on respect for the freedom of speech and expression, freedom of religion, freedom from need and freedom from fear[54].

The Declaration was approved with the assent of the world's powers, whose relations were in those very months rapidly deteriorating towards the Cold War. Had there been only weeks of delay, the Declaration might have never been completed.

Eleanor Roosevelt was the first frank, tenacious and polemical First Lady, and a woman who had lived through most of the 20th century's historical events. Over her life, she influenced world events as much as did her husband, President Franklin D. Roosevelt.

People either loved or hated Eleanor Roosevelt. Her supporters found her intelligent, brave and passionate, a woman of action who was always toiling to improve the world. Her critics considered her was a politically naïve and scandalously pretentious woman.

One thing is sure: as a First Lady, Eleanor Roosevelt was an absolute pioneer. She wrote a regular news column, she worked as a radio commentator, and she gave speeches at political and press conferences.

As a child she was almost pathologically shy, but she managed to learn how to deal with criticisms and a life on the world stage. Once

---

[53] Mary Ann Glendon, *Verso un mondo nuovo*, Liberilibri, Macerata, 2001, xvi (Italian translation of *A World Made New*, Random House, 2002).

[54] *The Public Papers and Addresses of Franklin D. Roosevelt, 1938-1950*, vol. 9, New York, Russell & Russell, 1969, p. 672

she wrote "Every woman in public life needs to develop skin as tough as rhinoceros hide"[55].

After her parents' death, young Eleanor was raised by her maternal grandmother, Mary Ludlow Hall. Eleanor thus lived in a rather hostile environment, also due to the presence of her future mother-in-law, Sara Delano Roosevelt. She complained about the situation to her aunt Anna "Bamie" Cowles (Theodore Roosevelt's sister), who decided to take her away from the Halls. Her uncle Ted welcomed her in his home, where, at a Christmas party, she met her distant cousin and future husband Franklin Roosevelt.

Encouraged by her aunt Bamie, she attended Allenswood, an all-girls school near London from 1899 to 1902. There she met Marie Souvestre, a teacher who was interested in liberal and feminist causes. Eleanor described her as one of the most influential people of her life. When it was time to go back to New York, Souvestre did her best to prepare Eleanor to enter the Roosevelt Family of Hyde Park.

In 1902 she began to date Franklin Delano, then a Harvard student; their dating turned into an engagement in November 1903. Sara Ann Roosevelt, Franklin's mother, was against the wedding, managed to have it postponed and sent her son on a 16-month trip with his friends to try and make him forget Eleanor. However, most of the family favored the union. The greatest support came from Uncle Theodore, who wrote a letter to Franklin to express his approval. On 17 March 1905, Eleanor and Franklin married; their union was to produce six children.

The mother of the future President of the United States considered Eleanor shy, not particularly attractive and inexperienced in life. Eleanor let Sara dominate the first years of her married life entirely, even though at the time of marriage her income was not much lower than her husband's, and the couple certainly did not need Sara's financial support.

The turning point in Eleanor's life came in 1921, when her husband contracted poliomyelitis and was paralyzed from the waist down. Eleanor finally stood up to her mother-in-law, who insisted

---

[55] Description of the movie program for *Eleanor Roosevelt, American Experience*, Public Broadcasting Service, www.pbs.org/wghb/amex/eleanor/filmmore/description.html.

that her son retire from political life and resign himself to his fate as a cripple. Eleanor managed to convince her husband to continue and became his "legs and ears", gaining a personal sphere of action. Eleanor's constant encouragement enabled Franklin to return to politics and become the Governor of New York (1929-1933).

After Franklin won the Governorship, Eleanor began to participate in his visits to homes, hospitals and prisons in her own name. She also worked for the League of Women Voters, the National Consumers League, the Women's Trade Union League and the female section of the Democratic Committee of the State of New York.

When Franklin Delano Roosevelt was elected President of the United States (1933-1945), Eleanor Roosevelt became the first "activist" First Lady. With press conferences and a daily news column, she kept in touch with the public on the White House's social policies, especially the New Deal. She convinced her husband to create the National Youth Administration (NYA) to provide financial aid to students and professional training for young men and women.

Her concern for the disadvantaged Blacks of America led her to work closely with organizations such as the National Association for the Advancement of Colored People. In 1939 she resigned from the Daughters of the American Revolution organization to protest against its refusal to let the Black singer Marian Anderson sing in the Constitution Hall; she did when Washington was still ruled by segregation.

When Franklin D. Roosevelt died in 1945, Eleanor Roosevelt's role as a First Lady drew to an end. However, she did not retire to a private life. In 1947, the new President Harry S. Truman (1884-1972) asked her to become the United States Representative for the United Nations Commission on Human Rights, in a time when the horrors of the two World Wars were vivid memories.

At the age of sixty-two, she was about to reach the most important milestone of her already illustrious public life.

When President Truman asked her to become part of the United States Delegation to the United Nations, Eleanor Roosevelt wondered "how can I help in the United Nations when I have neither specific training nor any experience with international conferences?"[56]

---

[56] Eleanor Roosevelt, *On My Own*, New York, Harper, 1958, p. 39.

According to some foreign affairs professionals, there was also the risk that the ex-First Lady's famed candor could become a loose cannon in this new context. As a political activist and famous journalist, Eleanor had built an extraordinary reputation based on her independence of thought and determination in fighting for progressive causes. While at the White House, the First Lady had even used her news column to criticize some decisions taken by her husband's government, such as against a measure of the economic recovery plan that removed married women from work. Franklin Delano Roosevelt serenely accepted these public differences, and it is said that he once told his wife "My dear, this is a free country. Say what you think. If you put me in trouble, it will be up to me to get out. Anyway, the whole world knows that I do not control you"[57].

Looking back some months after the decision to accept Truman's proposal, Eleanor wrote to the readers of her news column:

"[I accepted this post] because I felt able to put my life experience to the service of my nation and of the peoples of the world, in this particular historical moment. I knew, of course, how much my husband hoped that once the war was over, an organization for peace would be really created. But I did not do it only to fulfill my husband's hopes [...] I did it instead because personally, I have always thought that women might have greater chances to foster the understanding necessary to prevent future wars if they could serve in international organizations in greater numbers"[58].

The human rights project was of only marginal importance; it was established as a concession to the smaller nations and in response to the calls advanced by several humanitarian and religious associations, which expected the Allies to live up to their wartime rhetoric and ensure that the community of nations would no longer tolerate such serious violations of human dignity. The States did not expect these guarantees to interfere with their national sovereignty.

"Many members of the Commission for Human Rights became the protagonists of a satirical comic that portrayed the United Nations dignitaries as a class of scholars and Mrs. Roosevelt as a teacher, who

---

[57] Blanche Wiesen Cook, *Eleanor Roosevelt, Volume 2: 1933-1938*, New York, Viking, 1999, pp. 7, 37, 74.

[58] See Allida M. Black (ed.), "Eleanor Roosevelt", in *What I Hope to Leave Behind: the Essential Essays of Eleanor Roosevelt*, Brooklyn, Carlson, 1995, p. 35.

said "Children, all together now: individual rights come before State rights". Some of the children look bored; many are misbehaving"[59].

Over the next few years, human rights surprisingly became a political factor that not even the strictest realist could ignore. The Universal Declaration became an instrument and at the same time, the clearest symbol, of the changes that were to amplify the voices of weaker States within the chambers of power. It thus served to defy the long-established opinion that the treatment accorded by sovereign State to its citizens concerns that country alone and no other.

Its thirty concise articles inspired and influenced a great number of post-war and post-colonial constitutions and treaties, and are the basis of a body of evolving international law that protects the rights of men and women throughout the world. The Declaration became the guiding star for an army of activists who fight for international human rights, who pressure governments to live up to the commitments they take and to publicize abuses that, in other times, would not have come to light.

The Universal Declaration of Human Rights became an important pillar of a new international system, in which the treatment given by a State to its citizens is no longer exempt from external control.

A declaration of the United Nations General Assembly takes the shape of a resolution; like any other congressional resolution, it does not have intrinsic legal force. Instead, conventions, pacts, and treaties are agreements through which nations assume legally binding obligations. These enter into force only after they are ratified and feature control mechanisms for their implementation.

Due to the strong resistance opposed by States, it was decided to transpose human rights into two separate legal documents. The first document was not to be binding upon States and was a manifesto on human rights for all human beings: the Universal Declaration of Human Rights.

The second was to be a convention that would be binding upon the States that chose to ratify it. Nineteen years would pass before the two human rights conventions, one on political and civil rights, and the other on economic, social and cultural rights, were submitted

---

59   Glendon, *op. cit.*, p. 86.

for the signature of Member States, and ten years more before these conventions received enough signatures to enter into force, in 1976. All the great powers fiercely defended their sovereignty.

Unable to reach a unanimous solution on which of the three proposals was to have priority, the majority of the Commission eventually accepted Fernand Dehousse's suggested compromise: the delegates decided to proceed at the same time in all three directions, and the Commission divided into three working groups, which prepared a Declaration, a Convention and implementing measures. The first group, presided by Mrs. Roosevelt, worked on the draft Declaration.

On 28 September 1948, in a famous speech, Eleanor Roosevelt proclaimed the Declaration to be the "international Magna Charta of all humanity, all over the world". She praised the Declaration as an important step in the endless task of raising human beings in all parts of the world "to a higher quality of life and to a greater chance of enjoying freedom". She added that it was based "on the spiritual fact that man must enjoy the freedom within which to fully develop his potential and, through a joint effort, raise the level of human dignity". The Declaration was approved almost unanimously by the General Assembly of the United Nations on 10 December 1948, with only eight abstaining votes. The Universal Declaration of Human Rights affirmed the international right to life, freedom and equality for all human beings, regardless of race, religion or color.

Eleanor Roosevelt worked until the end of her days to achieve the acceptance and implementation of the rights enshrined in the Declaration:

"Where, after all, do universal human rights begin? In small places, close to home—so close and so small that they cannot be seen on any maps of the world. Yet they are the world of the individual person; the neighborhood he lives in; the school or college he attends; the factory, farm, or office where he works. Such are the places where every man woman and child seeks equal justice, equal opportunity, equal dignity without discrimination. Unless these rights have meaning there, they have little meaning anywhere. Without concerted citizen action to uphold them close to home, we shall look in vain for progress in the larger world. We

therefore believe that the fate of human rights is in the hands of all the citizens in all our communities." ("In Your Hands" speech, 27 March 1958).

Today, the Declaration is the most important point of reference for international debates on how to plan our shared future on an interdependent, but ever more war-torn planet. However, time and oblivion have a price. Even within the international movement for human rights, the Declaration has begun to be considered more as a monument to be venerated from a distance rather than a living document that each generation must make its own. Indeed, rarely has a text been so universally praised and, at the same time, so little read or understood.

Eleanor Roosevelt understood these dangers. She often repeated that the documents that enshrine ideals "have no influence unless people know them, understand them and ask for their transposition into reality"[60].

Until we have a better instrument, as Mrs. Roosevelt once said of the UN, the Declaration is "a bridge upon which we can meet and talk"[61].

Eleanor was also interested in foreign policy. After the United States entered World War II (1939-1945) in 1941, she often traveled to the front to support the Red Cross' activities and to boost the troops' morale.

In 1943, with Wendell Willkie and other United States figures, she laid the foundations for the establishment of "Freedom House", a research institute for the promotion of peace and democracy in the world. Eleanor managed to collect a large amount of funds.

She wrote several books on her experiences: *This is my story* (1937), *This I Remember* (1950), *On My Own* (1958) and *Tomorrow Is Now* (published posthumously, 1963).

In 1962, Eleanor was also part of the Presidential Commission on the Condition of Women, presided by John F. Kennedy. Eleanor

---

[60] Black, *op. cit.*, p. 559 (Eleanor Roosevelt's speech entitled *Making Human Rights Come Alive*).

[61] Eleanor Roosevelt, the U.N. and the Wlefare of the World, "National Parent-Teacher" 47, 1953, 14.

Roosevelt's feminism was passionate but pragmatic. She gave women's suffrage the merit of having forced governments to concern themselves with the well-being of humanity, and sought to prove, through her efforts, that greater participation of women in political and economic life could make a difference. For her, this meant helping those who were still politically and economically emarginated.

For Eleanor Roosevelt, this was a women's job—she believed that these issues would remain neglected unless women championed them. It seemed to her that men in power, including even men like her husband, did not devote themselves enough to dealing with the country's social ills. As highlighted by her biographer Blanche Wiesen Cook, the First Lady's aim was to reach out to all the women of America and to convince them that "it was their task to take on these problems, to organize and work for social progress"[62]. Eleanor wished to see ever more women work together in governments and private organizations to define the country's policies, on an equal basis with men[63].

As for women's rights, Mrs. Roosevelt was decidedly in favor of equal opportunities, both in the workplace and in public life.

However, she asserted with equal strength that there were certain areas, such as children's education and military service, where it was necessary to take into account the differences between the sexes.

She did not believe that the roles of father and mother were interchangeable. She believed that mothers, as principal educators of their children, played a special role in forging the nation's destiny. She believed that the majority of women, whether mothers or not, had a common particular interest in children's welfare: "there exist some fundamental things that are more important for the majority of women than they are for the majority of men. These are certainly connected to women's biological functions. Women carry children in their wombs and love them even before they are born [. . .]. We can find a more or less strong interest for children in women who have never had children. Thus ensues their interest for the home, which is

---

[62] Cook, *op. cit.*, p. 75.
[63] Eleanor Roosevelt, *My Day*, 28 January 1946.

the place where children find shelter. And this is the great element of unity for most women"[64].

In 1962, she declared to the readers of *My Day*: "Naturally, the effort lies in seeking the best way to use women's potential without affecting their primary responsibilities, which are towards their homes, their husbands, and their children. We need to use in the best way possible the entire workforce available—including the female workforce—and I believe that this Commission will be able to show some of the ways in which this can be achieved."[65]

Eleanor lived through some of the most crucial events of the 20th century: the Great Depression, World War II, the creation of the United Nations and the adoption of the Universal Declaration of Human Rights. She faced opportunities and adversity with a spirit of optimism and determination. Once, Adlai Stevenson, a Democratic Presidential candidate, said of Eleanor Roosevelt that "she would rather light a candle than curse the darkness".

Even though her participation in the Declaration's actual formulation was limited, it is hard to imagine that the document could have been achieved without her. As President of the Commission for Human Rights, Eleanor Roosevelt gave the project the momentum it needed; by giving her personal attention, she made each member of the Commission feel respected. She represented and used the influence of her country, which had emerged from the war as the most powerful in the world. She nurtured the creation of better conditions for intercultural collaboration in every way, and gave her own personal touch to the spirit that informed the "new world" envisaged in the Declaration.

Seeking to explain her eminence, E. J. Kahn wrote, the year of the Declaration's adoption: "in times marked by the defense of self-interest both by nations and individuals, Mrs. Roosevelt has always distinguished herself as a person endowed with exceptional altruism". And citing an anonymous source with influential international contacts: "Mrs. Roosevelt never cares whether she receives any

---

[64]   Eleanor Roosevelt, *Women in Politics*, in Allida M. Black (ed.), *Courage in a Dangerous world*, p. 69.

[65]   *Ibid*, p. 299.

personal gain. She feels no pride for her position, nor personal ambition.

"But there is more: many Americans who have neither the time, the energy, her contacts, nor her skills, look upon her profuse efforts to improve the lives of her peers as the sort of thing that they wish they could do themselves, if only they were able to or had the means. For them—and I believe they are a great many—Eleanor is the embodiment of the American conscience"[66].

---

[66]   Glendon, *op. cit.*, p. 354.

CHAPTER **10**

CRYSTAL LEE SUTTON

(North Carolina, 31 December 1940-North
Carolina, 11 September 2009)

Trade union representative who fought for female workers' rights

Crystal Lee Sutton worked in a cotton factory in the South of the United States. In the early 1970s, a textile worker earned less than $2.80 per hour and worked six days a week.

Sutton was in charge of choosing the cotton, an 11th-category position in Roanoke Rapids in North Carolina, when she obtained her first job at J.P. Stevens & Co. for the 4 p.m.-to-midnight shift. Her task was to insert thread spools into fast looms.

There were seven cotton factories in her city. All belonged to one company, for which her grandparents and her parents had also worked. J.P. Stevens & Co. also owned several shotgun houses. Working in the textile industry was, therefore, almost inevitable.

When Sutton contacted the Textile Workers Union of America in Roanoke Rapids, she was thirty-two, a mother of three children and at her second marriage. Her first husband had died in a car accident when she was only 20, and had a four-month-old son.

As Crystal Lee Sutton told Henry P. Leifermann, author of *Crystal Lee: A Woman of Inheritance*, when she saw a trade union poster on a wall of the cotton factory in 1973, she was already thinking of the paltry wages, the backbreaking work and the exiguous earnings that she and her parents had endured. She wanted something better for her children.

The next day, she went to the first trade union meeting, which was held in an only-black church. Sutton was one of the two whites present. She wore a red and white five-inch-wide pin that said "I am with TWUA". To her work at the factory, she brought a book entitled "What the Company can do for you", the pages of which were entirely blank. From that moment, she decided to hold the trade union meetings at her own home and to talk to hear colleagues about it before and after work, and during her 30-minute break. Eli Zivkovich, sent by TWUA to organize the Roanoke Rapids trade union, later declared that during his twenty years as a trade unionist he had never met anyone as zealous as Sutton. Not everyone at Roanoke Rapids was convinced though, and some did not approve of her. The South's textile workers had a long history of resistance to organized labor; they had imbibed anti-trade union rhetoric since childhood, from the pulpits to their schoolrooms. For many, trade unions were an instrument of black power; the victory of trade unions would lead to the closing of all factories.

In May 1973, Zivkovich asked Sutton to copy a letter against trade unions that had been published on the factory's noticeboard, that declared, among other things, that blacks would run the trade union. This was dangerous, as the supervisors had warned workers not to copy information from the noticeboards. Also, they were anxious to find any excuse to get rid of Sutton.

One evening during a work break, Sutton took her notepad and stood in front of the noticeboard. Two supervisors were immediately behind her and were soon joined by another. They ordered her to stop writing, but she did not listen to them. When the general manager told her that she would be fired and he was going to call the police, Sutton continued anyway until she had finished copying the whole letter. Then she hid the sheet of paper in her bra.

The police was coming. When Sutton went towards her workstation, she saw a police officer come towards her. Knowing that she had only a few minutes left, she grabbed a black marker and a piece of cardboard. She wrote the words "TRADE UNION" and stood on her workstation, holding the sign over her head with both hands. She slowly turned around, so that the whole room, full of hemmers and warehouse workers, could see her. Dozens of workers stopped what they were doing and stared. Many made a "V" for victory sign with their hands. Others raised their fists in the air. In 1979, Sally Field re-enacted that moment in an emblematic scene of the movie "Norma Rae", which was inspired by Sutton's life[67]. Sutton was taken away by the police, but the impact of her actions was fundamental. The Trade Union of Textile Workers of America obtained the right to represent the factory's workers on 28 August 1974. Crystal Lee officially became part of the TWUA trade union. She was the thirteenth winner of the *Pacem in Terris Peace and Freedom* Prize in 1980. The Prize is named after Pope John XXIII's 1963 encyclical *Pacem in Terris*, which exhorts men of goodwill to work for peace between nations.

However, one more year was to pass before trade unions obtained the right to represent workers, and seven more years before J.P. Stevens & Co. signed a contract with the trade union for three thousand workers at Roanoke Rapids. The new 1980 contract raised wages to averagely $5 per hour, introduced health and safety policies and established new seniority rules. Although Sutton was not the only worker who was decisive in ensuring the Union's success, her determination on that evening of May 1973 certainly injected new courage into the struggle.

Over the next few years, Sutton continued to work in various underpaying jobs in the kitchen of a fast-food restaurant. In the early 1980s, she traveled throughout the United States as a spokeswoman for the trade union.

After she was dismissed from J.P. Stevens, she stood outside the factory day after day with other supporters, distributing the union's leaflets and pins. When the workers filed past her to go to work, in jeans and a TWUA t-shirt she would say with a Southern accent, both sweet and firm, "hey, please sign the union's membership card", "I'll stand here 'til you sign the card".

Crystal Lee Sutton died of a brain tumor at the age of sixty-eight, in a hospital in Burlington, North Carolina. It was September 11, 2009. She had struggled against her health insurance company, which had delayed the treatment of her illness.

THE 1968 DAGENHAM STRIKE FOR EQUAL RIGHTS

---

[67] The movie *Norma Rae* is based on the first years of Sutton's work as a trade union official. The film is based on the book written by Henry Hank Leiferman, a *New York Times* journalist, entitled *Crystal Lee: A Woman of Inheritance* and published in 1975.

In summer 1968, around 200 female workers went on strike at the Ford Motors factory in Dagenham, England, to protest against the discrimination they suffered. The strike brought the issue of women's rights in factories to public attention, and eventually led to the enactment of an important piece of legislation for equal pay in the United Kingdom. The 187 women in Dagenham worked at sewing machines to create the upholstery of many car models produced by Ford. They protested because they had been placed in the trade union's "B" grade of unqualified workers, while men who performed their same work had been placed in the "C" grade, for semi-qualified workers. Women also received less pay than men, even men who were in the B grade and whose task was to sweep the factory's floors. The strike paralyzed production completely, since Ford could not sell cars without seats, and helped the women and their supervisors to understand how essential their work was.

At first, the trade union did not support the strike. Strategies to divide the workers were often deployed, to avoid men supporting an increase in women's wages. According to the Dagenham workers, the prospect of losing the membership of the 187 women did not worry the trade union leaders at all, as the union assisted hundreds of other workers. The women pursued their struggle nevertheless; soon, other 195 women of another Ford factory in the UK joined them.

The Dagenham strike ended when the then-Secretary of State for Employment Barbara Castle met the women and pushed for their reinstatement. The women received a raise, but the issue of their job classification was solved only some years later, after another strike in 1984, when they were finally classified as qualified workers.

Female workers throughout England benefited from the Dagenham strike, as it led to the Equal Pay Act 1970, the law that makes it illegal to establish separate pay levels for men and women, as these are impermissibly based on sexual discrimination.

CHAPTER 11

SHIRIN EBADI

(Hamadan, 21 June 1947-)

Muslim lawyer who fought for the rights of Iranian women

SHIRIN EBADI SPEAKS ON ISLAMIC FEMINISM. PRESS CONFERENCE—BRUSSELS—MARCH 2nd, 2009—MEETING ORGANIZED BY WWW.MO.BE AND BROADCAST BY WWW.SHAHRZADNEWS.ORG[68]

JOURNALIST: We would like Ms. Ebadi to speak to us about women and their rights in Iran, and especially about the women's movements and the organization of the Islamic feminist movement of which we have heard.

SHIRIN EBADI: Actually, I am contrary to the concept of "Islamic feminism", as I am against that of "Islamic rights of man", in the sense that the rights of man cannot be based on exclusively Islamic principles, or in any case conceived through Islam. I am also against this concept of "Islamic democracy". Concepts such as women's rights, feminism, the rights of man, democracy, equality, are concepts and notions with a universal meaning; in both the East and the West they have the same meaning.
Their definition does not change if one is in an Islamic or Muslim country. Therefore, when we speak of Islamic feminism and Islamic democracy, these are concepts that are not very distant from the original concepts of feminism and democracy. A Muslim woman can be a feminist. I myself am Muslim and a feminist. Indeed, Islam possesses an intrinsic impartiality necessary for enabling women's equality. We must have a

---

68   Translated from French into Italian by Rosanna Damato.

modern perception and perspective of Islam, to show that this equality, equality for a feminist Muslim woman, is possible. However, it is incorrect to speak of Islamic feminism."

"For most of my younger years—as happens with all the children for whom the family is the only known world—I did not realize that my family was special. The fact that my parents treated my brother no differently from my sisters was not striking to me. It all seemed perfectly natural and I assumed that it happened everywhere. However, it was not at all the case. In the great majority of Iranian families, male children enjoy a special status [. . .] In Iranian culture, it was considered natural for fathers to love their male children more, upon whom the family's future hopes were pinned. In my home, our parents divided attention, affection and discipline equally. Our parents treated us impartially. It was only when I was an adult that I understood that my ideal of gender equality and my self-confidence was chiefly thanks to the example I had received at home. My father's support of my independence, from my childhood games to my decision to become a judge, instilled in me a faith in my own capabilities that I was never consciously aware of, but that in the end I consider as his most precious legacy"[69].

Shirin Ebadi was born on 21 June 1947, the summer before her family left Hamadan for Tehran. With Mossadeq's defeat, her father, a longtime supporter, was forced to leave his job. Before the coup, he had been proposed for the post of Vice-Minister of Agriculture. For many years, he occupied lower positions, and was never again nominated for a higher job.

Shirin wrote that the Prime Minister Muhammad Mossadeq was not merely an ex-statesman, but one of the greatest Iranian leaders to guide Iran during the first stirrings of democracy in its history. The old Prime Minister died for natural causes but was much mourned as a great hero and martyr, as if he had fallen in an epic battle. From the day of his death, her father refused to talk about politics at home.

In 1965, Ebadi enrolled in the School of Law. She began to frequent the campus and intellectual environment of the University

---

[69]   Shirin Ebadi, *Il mio Iran*, Sperling & Kupfer, 2007, pp. 11-13 (English title: *Iran Awakening*, New York, Random House, 2006).

of Tehran with the dream of becoming a judge. The student demonstrations there alerted the Savak, the Shah's secret police, which combed the campus ceaselessly. A massive police apparatus was put in place, to hunt for those who were organizing insurrections against the regime.

In March 1970, at the age of twenty, Shirin Ebadi became a judge. At the swearing-in ceremony, attended by the Minister of Justice, high-ranking judges and professors of the School of Law, the two best students had to carry a huge Quran to the stage: "I was very short, and the other student was very tall. In the end, we managed to pull the heavy sacred book to its destination and I delivered my speech. I read the oath and the other students repeated it after me. We then came down from the stage and went towards what we thought with all our hearts would be a life devoted to serving justice."

"On a clear, cold spring morning of 1975, a young engineer called Javad Tavassolian entered my courtroom and approached me, with the excuse of asking my opinion on some difficult legal issues. He wore an elegant ivory-colored suit and a brown shirt, and stayed a while to chat with me. [. . .] After several informal meetings, over coffee or ice-cream, he asked me to marry him. [. . .] When the courtship period ended, we stopped seeing each other for a month, as we had agreed. The thirty days of distance gave us some time to think. We decided that ours was not just a crush or a friendship, but a profound conviction that a life together would work. Javad's family came to my parents' house, in accordance with tradition. [. . .]

My family held an *aghd-konoon*, a wedding celebration, in our house; together with our closest friends and our families, we gathered before the *sofreh aghd*, the nuptial banquet. The Attorney General of Tehran was one of our witnesses, and he was late. While we waited for him, my mother noticed, to her great anxiety, that the Quran on the banquet table was much too small. At that very moment, the Attorney General arrived, bearing as a wedding gift an elegant Quran of the right size. I thought to myself that it was a truly auspicious sign, and I placed the book at the center of the laden table. The married and unmarried women of the family held over our heads an embroidered canopy, from which they shook sugar wrapped in muslin to wish sweetness to our union. Javad was thirty-three, and I was twenty-eight"[70].

---

70 *Ibid.*, p. 31.

Shirin Ebadi began working at the Ministry of Justice while the Government was persecuting its critics in martial courts and held trials outside of the public legal system. In military tribunals, dissidents faced the vague and generic charges—sabotage, danger to national security, etc.—that repressive regimes use for any activity considered threatening.

She was removed from her position as a judge at a meeting in the Tehran district court, in late 1980. It was a full-fledged dismissal, since the men of the expurgation committee did not even invite her to sit down, even though she was six months pregnant. The men were seated around a wooden table. Two were judges she knew well, and one had been her subordinate until the previous year. One judge instructed her to "come to the legal office when you have finished your leave". The "legal office" was where civil servants worked. The instruction meant that she was being downgraded to the job of clerical worker and typist.

Over the next few days, Ebadi went to the legal office at 9 a.m. sharp. But from the day of her arrival, she announced that, since she had been downgraded against her will, she refused to perform any work in protest. Every day, she went to her office and just sat at her desk. One day she read an unbelievable article on the newspaper *Enghelab-e Eslami* ("Islamic Revolution"), on the introduction of a penal code based on Islamic law. This would have changed the very foundations of government, the relations between citizens and the law, the organizational principles and the social contracts upon which collective life was based.

These dark laws, against which she would fight for the rest of her life, included the following: the value of a woman's life is half that of a man (so for example, if a car runs over both in a road accident, the compensation due to the man's family would be double that of the woman's family); a woman's witness statement in court counts half that of a man; a woman must obtain her husband's permission before divorcing. In other words, the new laws turned the emancipation clock back by 1400 years, or the beginning of Islam's diffusion.

Some days later, a group of professors of the University of Tehran's School of Law wrote a letter of protest, stating that the new penal code was entirely out of place in the 20th century and that it should not enter into force. They were immediately removed from their positions and suspended, but the shortage of professors led to their gradual reinstatement.

"The day that Javad and I married, we united as equal individuals. But now, with those laws, he remained a person and I became a movable good. He was allowed to divorce on a whim, take the custody of our children, marry three more wives".

Shirin Ebadi asked her husband to sign a post-nuptial agreement in which he guaranteed her right to divorce and, in this case, the possibility to have the custody of their children. On 21 April 1980, five years after meeting, their daughter Negar was born. Ebadi "worked" in the legal office almost until her labor started. Then, she says, "I stayed at home for two months, to look at that mysterious pink creature, to dry her saliva and to massage her back through her rompers so that she could burp. She had seduced me completely, and not only because her infant world, the soothing lullabies and the rituals to prepare her food were a break from the ugliness of the outside world, the executions and the constantly rising expurgations"[71].

When she resumed working, the atmosphere had become even more oppressive and intimidating. A new iniquitous and arbitrary law was approved almost every day. Nobody dared protest for fear of being labeled anti-Islamic. A while later, a law was enacted to establish that only men could be judges, and that all female judges had to be assigned to administrative jobs. Ebadi was appointed the the secretary of what had once been her courtroom.

"Of course, the great majority of us female judges did not keep quiet. We protested wherever possible: in the corridors, with friends who had connections among the revolutionaries, with the new minister".

On 22 September 1908 Saddam Hussein invaded Iran and launched the "*qadisiya*"[72] against the country, the Arab-Muslim invasion of what had once been Persia.

---

[71] *Ibid.*, p. 68.

[72] From the name of the place where, in 636 CE, the Arab troops defeated the army of the Persian Empire and thus gave rise to the spread of Islam in the Iranian plateau and Central Asia.

Khomeini openly displayed his determination to spread the Shi'a revolution throughout the region. His revolutionaries believed that Islam had no borders and that nationalism, compared to faith, was a worldly, vile attitude. They considered the region ranging from Lebanon to Iraq as fertile grounds for the birth of an Islamic *Shi'a* ("party") that would erase all the boundaries artificially drawn by the British colonizers. The ayatollah defined the fight as an externally-imposed war, likening it to an ancient struggle that the *Shi'a* had led against despotism. He compared Saddam to Yazid, the evil Shi'ite who had killed Imam Hussein, the Shi'ite saint and nephew of the Prophet Muhammad, during the battle of Kerbala.

Saddam had the advantage of access to Western military arsenals, from which he acquired chemical agents and weapon stocks. Iran, on the other hand, was the most populous nation of the region.

Shirin Ebadi continued to work in her usual post, but she had been given a new task as "specialist" in the department for the protection of children and the mentally ill, within the Public Prosecutor's Office of Tehran. The department assigned legal guardians to the legally incapable and to children without fathers or grandfathers. Every day, mothers would come to her and ask for the legal custody of their children. The new office was right in front of the courtyard where celebrations in honor of war victims were held.

On April 30, 1982, around forty thousand youths, armed with profound faith and rusty Kalashnikovs, crossed the Arvand River and entered the mined fields. The capture of Khorramshahr, a strategic port that crossed the southern part of the river that separates Iran from Iraq, had been a real shock for the Iranian defense as it was the only important city to have fallen in Saddam's hands. That night, the Iranian commanders led their men into the heart of the two fully-armored enemy battalions and fought hard to take the city from the Iraqi troops.

During the first and second stages of the battle, waves of Iranian soldiers entered the city suburbs, defying heavy air raids, and freed many areas; in the third stage, they built a bridge over the river and surrounded the main road ringing the city for the final assault. On May 24, the Iranians marched triumphantly through the city streets; they took twelve thousand Iraqi prisoners. Khorramshahr saw so much blood that the ayatollah Khomeini renamed it "Khooninshahr", the city of blood. When his soldiers proclaimed victory, he said "It was God who freed Khorramshahr".

The battle of Khorramshahr was a political and military turning-point: "We had recovered our territory and Saddam realized that he could not defeat an enemy that would continue to send actual human waves. It was assumed, with much relief, that the war was about to end. Indeed, the following month the Iraqi dictator proposed an armistice".

It had again become compulsory to wear the veil, but Shirin often forgot. "Usually, before opening the door I would look around the living room quickly, with the impression of having forgotten something. Once I went out and noticed that passers-by kept turning to look at me. 'Mrs. Ebadi', one neighbor finally dared to shout, 'you forgot your *hijab!*' I ran back home and tied a cotton scarf around my head. That evening I told a friend on the phone 'if a policeman had seen me, I would have been arrested'".

In 1983, her second daughter Nargess (narcissus).

It is impossible to estimate with any reliability the cost of war for the populations of Iran and Iraq and the two countries' economies. Both sides faced costs of about five hundred billion US dollars, including forsaken income from the sale of petroleum, military expenditure and destroyed infrastructure. Tehran and Baghdad agreed on one point only: over one million Iranians and Iraqis had been killed or injured. About one hundred thousand soldiers had been captured, and the war had created 2.5 million refugees.

After the first two years of the post-war phase, the Islamic Republic changed its course. The government leaders concluded that Iran had to reintegrate into the world economy or it would have regressed. Privatization, greater focus on the manufacturing industry rather than agriculture, and the attraction of new foreign investors became the country's priority. Society had to be rebuilt after the devastating war, and all forces, including females, were needed.

A consequence of this involuntary pragmatism was a "relaxing" of the judicial system; in 1992, Ebadi regained her authorization to practice law. She set up an office in the ground-floor apartment of the building where she lived and began to receive clients. Her days were filled with commercial and financial cases, although occasionally, when politics-related cases reached her, she worked on a *pro bono* basis. Soon enough, after attending court with her clients and having discussed a number of cases, she realized that the justice being administered was justice in name only. She thought that commercial disputes at least would not be permeated by the politics and the ideology of the new Islamic Republic. "As a lawyer, it was my duty to promote the cause of my client, help him to recover the money or property, or defend him from unfair accusations. More than once, a client would come to my office, radiant, pleased to inform me that the claimant had agreed to let the issue go in return for a bribe. What then was the use of knowing the law and preparing a defense? Or rather, what was the use of appearing in court, pretending to follow the legal procedure, when everything was really solved in the judge's office with a bribe? On two occasions, finding nothing more to say, the judge declared that some locks of my hair had slipped out from my *hijab* and adjourned the hearing due to my inappropriate dress".

Having managed previously without two incomes, thought Ebadi, she could go on like this. Indeed, she did not just work to earn but especially to feel fulfilled, to apply her professional skills and to contribute to her country. First she accepted commercial cases, but found that she was abandoning her principles. She thus decided to take on only *pro bono* work, as that would allow her to expose the iniquities of the judicial system.

Shirin Ebadi thus chose cases that exemplified the tragic repercussions of the theocracy's discrimination against women. "I wrote an article for the *Iran-e Farda* magazine in a language that was easily comprehensible rather full of technical jargon; that could express in clear terms the inferior status of women in the Iranian Penal Code, explaining how outrageous these laws were and how they considered women as 'non-persons'. The article electrified the educated classes of Tehran. The magazine's director enthusiastically published it. The issue ran out in the blink of an eye and people kept going to the magazine's offices for at least a photocopy. I was stunned. I had not expected that it would have such a great impact on the entire city. A hardline Member of Parliament publicly threatened me, telling journalists: "Somebody stop that woman, or we will silence her". When I heard these words, I understood for the first time that the system feared me and the public's growing interest for my work"[73].

In the meantime, Shirin Ebadi's visibility grew: "You work, you talk, you write articles and hold conferences, you meet clients and defend them, day after day. Then one morning, you wake up and realize that you have come a long way, that you have built a reputation. That is what happened to me.

On the personal level, I was not really affected, but then I realized that it was an extremely positive thing. It meant that journalists would listen to me if I spoke to them of a case I was following, and that they would help me to publicize it in Iran and overseas. It meant that human rights observers throughout the world knew me and trusted me, and that consequently they would launch serious appeals for the urgent cases that I brought to their attention. It meant that now in Iran there was a name and a face connected to the abstract expression 'human rights', and that millions of women who could not find their own words to express their frustration and their wishes had someone to speak in their name. After 1997, the moderate President Khatami tried to reduce significantly the political and religious system's interference with citizens' private lives.

In 2000, she was accused with false evidence of conspiring against the regime, as she had prepared a file on the wrongs committed by the paramilitary forces allegedly hired by the authorities to quell rebellions. Shirin Ebadi was imprisoned in the Evin jail in Tehran for twenty days, trialed and released on bail for twenty million *tomans* (€20.000).

In September 2003, Shirin Ebadi was invited to Paris to participate in a seminar on her country. At first, the Iranian Embassy in France objected to her involvement, stating that her opinions contrasted with the Government's official line: "it seemed like the system believed it was possible to control what was said and thought about Iran even overseas, and considered the visions different from its own to be illegitimate. The Embassy threatened to prevent the Iranian movies and works of art that were meant to be presented during the seminar from leaving the country, if I participated. The administrative authorities of Paris which had organized the seminar held their ground, until the Iranian Government finally backed down.

---

[73]   Ebadi, *op. cit.*, 269-274.

Some time before, I found out that my name had been on the list of candidates for the Nobel Peace Prize, but since an Iranian newspaper had reported that it had been removed, so I no longer thought about it. During my stay in Paris I never switched on the radio or the television".

However, Ebadi did win the Nobel Prize. Shirin Ebadi remembered the moment when she received the news: "that morning, our host bid us goodbye before he left for work. As we were approaching the door, the phone rang. A man introduced himself, saying that he had been tasked with calling me on behalf of the Committee for the Nobel Peace Prize. He told me to stay on the line because they had to give me some important news. I thought it was a prank, and hung up. Ten minutes later, another call came with the same message. I said that I had to go to the airport and was in a hurry, but my interlocutor insisted that it was important. When he understood that I did not believe him and that I was about to hang up again, he passed the phone to another person, who explained to me that I was a candidate for the prize. I heard someone in the background say that I had won the Nobel Peace Prize. I sat down, speechless with shock".

Ebadi was recommended to postpone her return home, as it was hard to predict how the Iranian Government would react. Also, in Tehran, journalists from the rest of the world would not be able to contact her easily, so it would have been better if she remained in France. In the space of two hours, a press conference was organized.

After the official communication that she had won the prize, a representative of the Iranian Embassy in Paris formally conveyed her the Ambassador's congratulations. He said that the Ambassador would have wanted to meet her, but as he had already made other commitments he would speak to her on the phone:

"I began to reflect on the true significance of the Prize. I did not think for even one second that it had been given to me as an individual. A recognition of this sort could only be given to what a person's life symbolized, to the path they followed to reach a higher aim. In the last twenty-three years, from the day when I was deprived of the possibility of working as a judge to the years when I had fought in Tehran's revolutionary courts, I always repeated this refrain: an interpretation of Islam that is harmonious with equality and democracy is a true expression of faith. It is not religion that binds women, but the selective precepts of those who want to force them into isolation. That belief, along with the conviction that change in Iran must arrive peacefully, from within, supported my work".

"I do not harbor illusions as to be able to retire, because it would mean that Iran has changed and that there is no longer any need for people like me to protect citizens from their own government. If I will live to see that day, I will sit back and applaud the efforts of the next generation in the tranquil solitude of my garden. If that will not be, I will continue as I have always done, in the hope that ever more Iranian friends will come to my side".

CHAPTER 12

HILLARY RODHAM CLINTON

(Chicago, 26 October 1947-)

The rights of the children of the "Global Village"

"Our lives are a mix of different roles. Most of us are doing our best to find the right balance. For me, the balance is family, work and service". (Presidential campaign, 1992)

"Back in 1959, I wanted to become a professor or a nuclear physicist. Teachers were necessary to 'train young citizens' and without them you wouldn't have 'much of a country'. America needed scientists because the 'Russians have about five scientists to our one.' Even then, I was fully a product of my country and its time, absorbing my family's lessons and America's needs as I considered my own future. My childhood in the 1950s and the politics of the 1960s awakened my sense of obligation to my country and my commitment to service. College, law school and then marriage took me into the political epicenter of the United States."

"By the time I crossed the threshold of the White House, I had been shaped by my family upbringing, education, religious faith and all that I had learned before—as the daughter of a staunch conservative father and a more liberal mother, a student activist, an advocate for children, a lawyer, Bill's wife and Chelsea's mom."

"A political life, I've often said, is a continuing education in human nature, including one's own. My involvement on the ground floor of two presidential campaigns and my duties as First Lady took me to every state in our union and to seventy-eight nations. In each place, I met someone or saw something that caused me to open my mind and my heart and deepen my understanding of the universal concerns that most of humanity shares."

"The two Clinton terms covered not only a transforming period in my life but also in America's. My husband assumed the Presidency determined to reverse the nations' economic decline, budget deficits and the growing inequities that undermined opportunities for future generations of Americans.

I supported his agenda and worked hard to translate his vision into actions that improved people's lives, strengthened our sense of community and furthered our democratic values at home and around the world."[74]

Hillary Diane Rodham was born on 26 October 1947 to Dorothy Howell Rodham and Hugh E. Rodham. Her father was self-employed and her mother was a housewife who also cared for Hillary's two younger brothers. Hillary's mother's parents neglected her and divorced in 1927. They sent their children to live with their paternal grandparents in Alhambra, a small town east of Los Angeles. "Her grandfather, Edwin Sr., a former British sailor, left the girls to his wife, Emma, a severe woman who wore black Victorian dresses and resented and ignored [Dorothy], except when enforcing her rigid house rules."

In recalling her mother's childhood, Hillary wrote: "after her childhood experiences, my mother opened her heart to the less fortunate and began to develop a sense of social justice that she transmitted to my sibling and me. Her capacity to react and her love for life have inspired me, and have catalyzed my interest for helping ill-treated and neglected children.

My parents also pushed me to witness events personally, convinced as they were that second-hand knowledge was no substitute for experience. When we were still young, they brought my siblings and me to the Chicago slums and left us—especially the boys—to take a good look at the drunkards lying on the sidewalk. "Those men could have become doctors, or lawyers", they explained[75].

---

[74] Hillary Rodham Clinton, *La mia vita, la mia storia*, Sperling & Kupfer editori, Milan, 2003, IX-XI (Italian translation of *Living History*, New York, Simon & Schuster, 2003).

[75] *Ibid.*, p. 20.

Hillary grew up in Park Ridge, Illinois. She attended Wellesley College, staying in the same student accommodation with the same five friends for all four years of college; she later said that each of those girls became a woman whose friendship sustained and helped her over the years.

When Martin Luther King was assassinated, she participated in an enormous protest and mourning march in Post Office Square, Boston, with a black strap tied to her arm. Some Black female students founded Ethos, the campus' first African-American organization which would serve as a social network for Black female students and as a pressure group in relations with the University. After King's assassination, Ethos pushed the college to develop greater racial sensitivity and to admit more Black teachers and students.

Wellesley's efforts to admit Black people began to pay off in the 1970s.

Two months later, on 5 June 1968, Senator Robert F. Kennedy was assassinated. Clinton said that she "often wondered whether political life was worth all the suffering and the struggle it entailed, and we always answered that it was, if only—as another friend who loved the Kennedys would say—to 'stop the others from gaining power'".

While Hillary Clinton was working in Washington on a nine-week internship, during a meeting on the Vietnam War, Mel Laird justified the American involvement and strongly argued for more, broader, military action. During questions, Hillary Clinton, referring to President Eisenhower's caution on American participation in Asian conflicts, asked him why he thought that strategy could be successful: "Although we didn't agree, as our heated exchange demonstrated, I came away with a high regard for him and an appreciation for his willingness to explain and defend his views to young people. He took our concerns seriously and respectfully."[76]

At the end of her internship, Congressman Charles Goodell asked Clinton and some others to follow him to the Republican Convention in Miami, to support Governor Rockefeller's last-ditch attempt to defeat Richard Nixon for the candidacy to leadership of his party.

---

[76] *Ibid.*, p.45.

The entire staff worked in the "Rockefeller for President" suite, answering the phone and relaying messages between Rockefeller's emissaries and delegates.

Rockefeller was not elected, and Republican Richard Nixon won.

In her speech at Wellesley, Hillary spoke of the "inescapable duty of critical and constructive protest". Paraphrasing Anne Scheibner's phrase, she stated that "now the challenge lies in practicing politics as the art of making possible that which appears impossible".

She could not imagine that her speech would spark interest well beyond Wellesley. Journalists and television shows wanted to interview her and call her. She participated in Irv Kupcinet's program on a local Chicago channel and "Life" magazine wrote about her and another student activist, Ira Magaziner, who had given the graduation speech at Brown. Later, Ira was to hold an important position in the Clinton administration.

The praise and criticism turned out to be a foretaste of the future. Hillary left for a summer job in Alaska, washing plates in Mount McKinley National Park and gutting fish in Valdez.

She later recalled: "My job required me to wear knee-high boots and stand in bloody water while removing guts from the salmon with a spoon. When I didn't slime fast enough, the supervisors yelled at me to speed up. Then I was moved to the assembly packing line, where I helped pack the salmon in boxes for shipping to the large floating processing plant offshore. [...] During a visit to Alaska when I was First Lady, I joked to an audience that of all the jobs I've had, sliming fish was pretty good preparation for life in Washington."[77]

In the fall of 1969, Hillary Clinton began Yale Law School as one of the twenty-seven female freshmen in a course of 250 students. "This seems like a paltry number now, but it was a breakthrough at the time and meant that women would no longer be token students at Yale."

In 1970, during her second year at Yale, she decided to specialize on the relationships between the law and children, and to further her knowledge of child development by attending a course at the Yale

---

[77] *Ibid.*, p.55.

Child Study Center. She remained there for one year, attending case discussions and observing clinical sessions.

She pursued these activities alongside her duties at the Legal Services office of the New Haven Hospital. Here, Clinton advised doctors who were trying to understand whether a child's injuries had resulted from abuse and, if so, whether the child should be removed from his/her family and entrusted to the uncertain care of social workers. For Clinton, who came from a strong family and who was convinced of parents' rights to raise their children as they deemed appropriate, those were terrible decisions to take. However, faced with serious mistreatment, she concluded that some people do relinquish the duties of parenthood, and other people, preferably another family member, and as a last resort the State, should intervene to offer the child a chance to have a stable and loving home.

Her first scholarly article, entitled "Children under the law", was published in 1974 on the *Harvard Educational Review*. "It explores the difficult decisions the judiciary and society face when children are abused or neglected by their families or when parental decisions have potentially irreparable consequences, such as denying a child medical care or the right to continue school."

In 1970 Bill Clinton returned to Yale, after two years in Oxford on a scholarship. He met Hillary in the Yale law library: "Bill Clinton and I started a conversation in the spring of 1971, and more than thirty years later, we're still talking."

One evening, during a party, they met in the kitchen and talked about their plans after graduation. She still did not know where she would live nor what she would do, because her interest in children's and civil rights did not impose any particular path. Bill, instead, was certain of his future: he wanted to go back home, to Arkansas, and run for public office. He had worked for Senator George McGovern's presidential campaign.

In her autobiography, Hillary Clinton wrote that in the summer of 1972, she worked to collect information on the fact that the Nixon administration still granted fiscal immunity to private educational institutions that practiced racial segregation. These institutions had been established in the South to avoid integrated public schools, although they claimed that they only responded to parents' demands for private education; they had nothing to do with the imminent integration of public schools. Hillary went to Atlanta to meet the civil rights lawyers and activists who were collecting the evidence to prove that those institutions were created with the sole aim of eluding the constitutional mandate imposed by the US Supreme Court's judgments, especially *Brown v Board of Education*[78].

Hillary went to Dothan, in Alabama. She pretended to be a young mother who was about to move to the area and wanted to enroll her son in an all-white school.

She made an appointment with an administrator of the local private school, the Southeast Education Academy, to talk about her imaginary son's enrolment. She asked questions on the syllabus and on the student body composition; she was assured that no Black students would have enrolled.

Clinton then moved to Cambridge, Massachusetts, to work in the new Children's Defense Fund with Marian Wright Edelman. During this time, she researched the conditions of children held in prisons for adults; sometimes, these children had to share cells with adult criminals, which would have contributed to the impossibility of recovering them.

In New Bedford, Massachusetts, Hillary Clinton was involved in verifying disturbing statistical data: the number of children of schooling age was vastly different from the number of enrolled children. Indeed, it was discovered that some children had not been enrolled because of physical disabilities such as blindness or deafness, and that others stayed at home to babysit their younger siblings while their parents were at work. In her autobiography, Clinton tells the story of a young girl in a wheelchair, who told her that she wanted to go to school, but was unable to because of her disability.

The results of the research reached Congress; two years later, after strong pressure from the CDF and other major organizations, the Education for All Handicapped Children Act was enacted; according to this law, all children affected by physical, emotional and learning

---

[78] *Brown v. Board of Education* was a milestone judgment handed down by the Supreme Court of the United States on 17 May 1954, in which the unconstitutionality of racial segregation in schools was proclaimed. The case gave the impetus for the fight for the civil rights of blacks.

disabilities had to receive an education within the public school system.

At twenty-six, Hillary and other forty-four lawyers were involved in the investigation for Richard Nixon's investigation, analyzing documents and transcribing recordings.

Dagmar Hamilton, a lawyer and professor of political science at the University of Texas, researched English cases of impeachment, while Hillary analyzed American ones. The team of lawyers collected the evidence necessary for launching a case for Richard Nixon's impeachment.

Together with Joe Woods, a commercial law expert, she prepared draft procedural rules to be submitted to the House Judiciary Committee.

On 19 July 1974, the impeachment charges were presented. The House Judiciary Committee unanimously approved three of these: abuse of power, obstruction of justice and contempt of Congress. On August 9, 1974, the President resigned.

Clinton then taught criminal law and forensic practice, while she managed the advice center for legal aid and a project on prisons. In the meantime, she also helped Bill in his electoral campaign.

After her marriage to Bill Clinton on October 11, 1975, Hillary worked for Rose, the most famous law firm in Arkansas. She had met one of the partners, Vince Foster, while she was directing the legal aid clinic during law school. When she tried to send law students to court to represent poor clients, a 19th-century law was in force that allowed use of legal aid only if a client's personal fortune did not exceed ten dollars.

Her aim was to change the rules. To do so, she needed the help of the Arkansas Bar in financing the center, which would have allowed it to hire a full-time administrator and secretary and free the young lawyers' time to practice their courtroom skills. At the time, Vince Foster was the head of the commission that oversaw legal aid. He called many other important lawyers to help her, including Henry Woods, the State's most renowned trial lawyer, and William R. Wilson Jr., also one of the best lawyers in town. Judge Butt and Hillary appeared before the Executive Committee of the Arkansas bar and each presented their arguments. Thanks to Foster's recruits, the Committee voted in favor of financing Clinton's center and of modifying the law.

In another case, Clinton was asked to represent a couple that wanted to adopt the child they had fostered for the past two and a half years. Arkansas social services refused, invoking a policy that prevented foster parents from adopting. However, the couple had the financial resources required to seriously challenge that policy.

To that end, Clinton and her collaborators presented an expert witness statement on the stages of child development and on how children's emotional well-being depends on the constant presence of figures in its first years of life. The judge was convinced that the contract signed by the foster parents—in which they had agreed to refrain from transiting to adoption—was not to be applied if its conditions damaged the child's interest. The State of Arkansas did not appeal and the case was won, although the official policy did not change. Still, the judgment constituted a precedent, which the State ended up adopting.

In Arkansas, there was no state body for protecting the rights and interest of minors. Dr. Bettye Caldwell, a world-renowned professor specialized in child development at the University of Arkansas at Little Rock, asked Clinton to join her and other citizens concerned about children's conditions. Thus, the Arkansas Advocates for Children and Families was born; it continues today to fight in the interests of children.

In 1979, Clinton became a partner of Rose; she was the firm's first female partner.

While she continued to work with Marian Wright Edelman and the Children's Defense Fund, President Carter had appointed her to the Management Board of the Legal Services Corporation, the non-profit federal program created by Nixon to finance legal aid for the poor.

"Our daughter's birth was the most miraculous and awe-inspiring event in my life. Chelsea Victoria Clinton arrived three weeks early on 27 February 1980".

For four months, Clinton took care of young Chelsea full-time, although on a lower salary. As a partner, she continued to receive a base pay, but her overall wage depended on her fees, which of course dropped during her absence from work. After this experience, she fought to ensure for all parents the right to remain at home after giving birth and to enjoy adequate daily help upon reprising work. Indeed, Bill Clinton, when President, endorsed her first bill, the Family and Medical Leave Act, on this very subject.

Hillary Clinton also participated in a seminar on women's health organized by the World Health Organization in China.

"This is truly a celebration—a celebration of the contributions women make in every aspect of life: in the home, on the job, in the community, as mothers, wives, sisters, daughters, learners, workers, citizens and leaders [. . .] However different we may appear, there is far more that unites us than divides us. We share a common future. And we are here to find common ground so that we may help bring new dignity and respect to women and girls all over the world—and in so doing, bring new strength and stability to families as well."

To risk everything in that speech meant being clear on the injustice of the Chinese government's behavior. The leaders in Beijing had prevented NGOs—working for causes that ranged from prenatal care to microfinance—from holding a forum in the capital, the city of Huairou, forty kilometers north of Beijing, with little adequate infrastructure. Although never naming China or other nations, it was almost impossible to doubt which serious human rights violations were being mentioned.

"I believe that on the eve of a new millennium, it is time to break our silence. It is time for us to say here in Beijing, and the world to hear, that it is no longer acceptable to discuss women's rights as separate from human rights . . . For too long, the history of women has been a history of silence. Even today, there are those who are trying to silence our words.

The voices of this conference and of the women at Huairou must be heard loud and clear: It is a violation of human rights when babies are denied food, or drowned, or suffocated, or their spines broken, simply because they are girls.

It is a violation of human rights when women and girls are sold into the slavery of prostitution.

It is a violation of human rights when women are doused with gasoline, set on fire and burned to death because their marriage dowries are deemed too small.

It is a violation of human rights when individual women are raped in their own communities and when thousands of women are subjected to rape as a tactic or prize of war.

It is a violation of human rights when a leading cause of death worldwide among women ages fourteen to forty-four is the violence they are subjected to in their own homes by their own relatives.

It is a violation of human rights when young girls are brutalized by the painful and degrading practice of genital mutilation.

It is a violation of human rights when women are denied the right to plan their own families, and that includes being forced to have abortions or being sterilized against their will.

If there is one message that echoes forth from this conference, let it be that human rights are women's rights . . . and women's rights are human rights, once and for all."

"I ended the speech with a call to action to [. . .] improve educational, sanitary, legal and political opportunities for women. [. . .] What I didn't know at the time was that my twenty-one-minute speech would become a manifesto for women all over the world. [. . .] The reaction of the Chinese government was not so positive. I learned later that the government had blacked out my speech from closed-circuit TV in the conference hall, which had been broadcasting highlights of the conference."[79]

In 1996, Hillary Clinton published "It Takes a Village"[80] on the policies to solve the problems affecting minors. It quickly became a best-seller and won a Grammy Award.

"Many of my convictions on what is best for children and their families do not fall within any political or ideological category, and many of those whom I met during my book tour assured me that they thought the same. Those people wanted to speak of how difficult it was to find quality, affordable services for their children, of the need to raise them in a culture that all too often exalts bad behavior and distorts values, of the importance of good, affordable schools and colleges, and a lot of other issues that confronted parents in an ever-changing world. I was heartened by those conversations, and hoped

---

[79]   Clinton, *op. cit.*, pp. 372-375.

[80]   Hillary Rodham Clinton, *It Takes a Village*, London, Pocket Books UK, 2007.

that my book would contribute to nurturing a national dialogue on what was best for children."[81]

In the book, Clinton considers her own personal experience as a mother, and her work for children, recalling an African proverb: "To raise a child, one needs a whole village". According to Clinton, we live in an interdependent world where what children hear, see and learn will condition their future and influence our lives.

This is why parents too must be supported, so that they can become the best parents possible. However, children depend on other adults too: teachers, doctors, neighbors, pastors. All these figures contribute to raising children and can become positive role models.

Every child deserves the chance to make use of his or her God-given potential.

According to a study undertaken by Urie Bronfenbrenner, a psychologist at Cornell University, this approach can be considered the "village child" model of human development. Bronfenbrenner had been predicting for years that the problems thought to affect only disadvantaged children would soon affect the whole society. The Government must therefore do its part to reverse children's crisis, and to do so, it cannot withdraw from its historical obligations towards the poor and the weak. The national budget must be squared, but not to the detriment of children. They do not deserve to inherit our debts, and neither must they be denied the chance to have a standard of living that includes healthcare, a good education, a protected environment, safe roads and economic opportunities. After all, children are citizens too.

Other countries have understood that honoring the family by granting it an adequate amount of time to take care of children is not only a family right. It is useful for society but is also positive for employers, who reap the benefits of the increased loyalty and serenity of workers. In Germany, for example, mothers are guaranteed fourteen weeks of maternity leave (six weeks before and eight weeks after giving birth) at full wage. Mothers also have guaranteed work leave for the first three years of the child's life, for the first year they receive a maternity bonus equal to about one-fifth of German women's average salary. While these economic benefits are not

---

[81] *Ibid.*, p. 408.

enough to support most families, they remain useful supplements to family income.

Other European countries make similar provisions, some of which are open to both fathers and mothers. For example, in Sweden, couples receive fifteen months of guaranteed work and paid leave, to be shared between them. The salary is about 90% of the full amount for the first twelve months, and is reduced further only in the last three months. Few Swedish fathers make use of these features.

Very often, the best interest of children do not seem to be a priority in individual and national programs. The consequences are clear to all: children's potential gives way to spirit-crushing poverty, children's health is lost in unsustainable anxiety, children's hearts are lost in the divorce and custody fights, their futures entrusted to an overburdened foster system, their lives crushed by abuse and violence: our society is left to its own devices, if we fail children.

"Everywhere we look, children are attacked: violence and negligence, family breakups, the temptations of alcohol, smoking, sex, substance abuse, greed, materialism, spiritual void. These problems are not new, but have, in our times, grown disproportionately. How well we take care of our children, and of those of others, is not only an issue of morality; our own personal interest is involved too. No family is immune from the influence of the whole society. The future of children will be influenced by how other children were raised. It is necessary to reduce to a minimum the chances that a child will suffer by the hand of someone who, as a child, did not receive enough love or discipline, opportunity and responsibility."

In her book "It Takes a Village", Clinton addressed society, both parents and not, stating that what happens to children affects the present and the future of all; therefore, everyone has a role in the life of every child, because it takes a village to raise a child.

Hillary Clinton was elected Senator of the State of New York on 7 November 2000. She will be the first First Lady to be elected to the United States Senate and the first woman to be elected in the entire State of New York. She recalled:

"I was overwhelmed by the generosity and openness of New Yorkers, who listened to what I had to say, got to know me and took a chance on me. I was determined not to let them down. I joined Bill, Chelsea, my mother, and scores of supporters in a deluge of confetti and balloons.

Dozens of hugs and handshakes later, I stood at the podium to thank my supporters. I told them: 'Sixty-two counties, sixteen months, three debates, two opponents and six black pantsuits later, because of you, we are here!'"[82]

"For the past eight years, I had watched from above as Bill shared his vision for our country in this same building. On January 3, 2001, I stepped onto the floor of the Senate to swear to 'support and defend the Constitution of the United States against all enemies foreign and domestic . . . and faithfully discharge the duties of the office on which I am about to enter.' When I turned and looked to the gallery above me, I saw my mother, my daughter and my husband smiling at the newest senator from New York."[83]

Hillary Clinton is currently a Secretary of State in the Obama administration.

In her inauguration speech, she recalled the main international questions to be solved: nuclear weapons, the Middle East, climate change, Africa, terrorism, the relationship with the allies and the new emerging countries such as China, India, and Brazil, and a vision of interdependence between states for the development, progress and implementation of human rights.

The following is an excerpt from Hillary Clinton's speech as Secretary of State, as reported by Jason Horowitz in his article published on the Washington Post on 13 January 2009:

"(. . .) Always, and especially in the crucible of these global challenges, our overriding duty is to protect and advance America's security, interests, and values: First, we must keep our people, our nation, and our allies secure. Second, we must promote economic growth and shared prosperity at home and abroad. Finally, we must strengthen America's position of global leadership—ensuring that we remain a positive force in the world, whether in working to preserve the health of our planet or expanding dignity and opportunity for

---

[82]   *Ibid.*, p. 635-636.
[83]   *Ibid.*, p. 638.

people on the margins whose progress and prosperity will add to our own.

(. . .) we were already living in a profoundly interdependent world in which old rules and boundaries no longer held fast—one in which both the promise and the peril of the 21st century could not be contained by national borders or vast distances.

(. . .) Non-state actors fight poverty, improve health, and expand education in the poorest parts of the world, while other non-state actors traffic in drugs, children, and women and kill innocent civilians across the globe.

Now, in 2009, the clear lesson of the last twenty years is that we must both combat the threats and seize the opportunities of our interdependence. And to be effective in doing so we must build a world with more partners and fewer adversaries.

America cannot solve the most pressing problems on our own, and the world cannot solve them without America. The best way to advance America's interest in reducing global threats and seizing global opportunities is to design and implement global solutions. This isn't a philosophical point. This is our reality.

The President-Elect and I believe that foreign policy must be based on a marriage of principles and pragmatism, not rigid ideology. On facts and evidence, not emotion or prejudice. Our security, our vitality, and our ability to lead in today's world oblige us to recognize the overwhelming fact of our interdependence.

I believe that American leadership has been wanting, but is still wanted. We must use what has been called "smart power," the full range of tools at our disposal—diplomatic, economic, military, political, legal, and cultural—picking the right tool, or combination of tools, for each situation. With smart power, diplomacy will be the vanguard of foreign policy. (. . .)"

I assure you that, if I am confirmed, the State Department will be firing on all cylinders to provide forward-thinking, sustained diplomacy in every part of the world; applying pressure and exerting leverage; cooperating with our military partners and other agencies of government; partnering effectively with NGOs, the private sector, and international organizations; using modern technologies for public outreach; empowering negotiators who can protect our interests while understanding those of our negotiating partners. There will be thousands of separate interactions, all strategically linked and coordinated to defend American security and prosperity. Diplomacy is hard work; but when we work hard, diplomacy can work, and not just to defuse tensions, but to achieve results that advance our security, interests and values. (. . .)

We must remember that to promote our interests around the world, America must be an exemplar of our values. Senator Isakson made the point to me the other day that our nation must lead by example rather than edict. Our history has shown that we are most effective when we see the harmony between our interests abroad and our values at home. And I take great comfort in knowing that our first Secretary of State, Thomas Jefferson, also subscribed to that view, reminding us across the centuries: "The interests of a nation, when well understood, will be found to coincide with their moral duties."

So while our democracy continues to inspire people around the world, we know that its influence is greatest when we live up to its teachings ourselves. Senator Lugar, I'm going to borrow your words here, because you have made this point so eloquently: You once said that "the United States cannot feed every person, lift every person out of poverty, cure every disease, or stop every conflict. But our power and status have conferred upon us a tremendous responsibility to humanity."

Right after I was nominated a friend told me: "The world has so many problems. You've got your work cut out for you." Well, I agree that the problems are many and they are big. But I don't get up every morning thinking only about the threats and dangers we face. With every challenge comes an opportunity to find promise and possibility in the face of adversity and complexity. Today's world calls forth the optimism and can-do spirit that has marked our progress for more than two centuries.

Too often we see the ills that plague us more clearly than the possibilities in front of us. We see threats that must be thwarted; wrongs that must be righted; conflicts that must be calmed. But not the partnerships that can be promoted; the rights that can be reinforced; the innovations that can be fostered; the people who can be empowered.

After all, it is the real possibility of progress—of that better life, free from fear and want and discord—that offers our most compelling message to the rest of the world. (. . .)

The great statesman and general George Marshall noted that our gravest enemies are often not nations or doctrines, but "hunger, poverty, desperation, and chaos." To create more friends and fewer enemies, we can't just win wars. We must find common ground and common purpose with other peoples and nations so that together we can overcome hatred, violence, lawlessness, and despair. (. . .)

In recent years, as other nations have risen to compete for military, economic, and political influence, some have argued that we have reached the end of the "American moment" in world history. I disagree. Yes, the conventional paradigms have shifted. But America's success has never been solely a function of our power; it has always been inspired by our values.

With so many troubles here at home and across the world, millions of people are still trying to come to our country—legally and illegally. Why? Because we are guided by unchanging truths: that all people are created equal; that each person has a right to life, liberty, and the pursuit of happiness. And in these truths we will find, as we have for more than two centuries, the courage, the discipline, and the creativity to meet the challenges of this ever-changing world.

I am humbled to be a public servant, and honored by the responsibility placed on me by our President-Elect, who embodies the American Dream not only here at home but far beyond our shores.

CHAPTER 13

JODY WILLIAMS

(Putney, Vermont, USA, 1950)

Leading the ban on landmines

From Cheryl Zechmann's interview of Jody Williams on YouTube (31 May 2011)

"Zechmann: If appointed Empress of the Universe [. . .] what would be the first thing you would change?

Williams: I would disband every army in the world. I would take all of that money, I would decide, with the people of communities around the world, how they want it to be used for their communities. I can't tell them what they need, they need to tell me as the Empress what they want to do with that money. Everybody has to be accountable. I'm not going to do the billions of dollars in duffle cases that we have squandered in Iraq and other countries. I'd listen to them. Why would I go tell anybody how to do what they need to do? They'll tell me, and I'll have some clever people who would help."[84]

When landmines are buried, they do not distinguish between soldiers and civilians who tend the fields, a woman looking for firewood to prepare lunch, a playing child. Also, once peace has been declared, mines continue to kill.

In Cambodia, there are today between four and six million landmines over 50% of the territory. Afghanistan's soil is seeded with about 9 million mines. In the few years of the ex-Yugoslavian conflict, about six million landmines were placed in various parts of

---

[84]   Transcript of an interview of Jody Williams by Cheryl Zechmann of 31 May 2011, posted on YouTube, www.youtube.com/watch?v=MnXEjagrqVk.

the country; there are nine million in Angola, and one million in Mozambique and in Somalia.

The International Red Cross has pressured governments around the world to increase restrictions on weapons considered excessively destructive; however, support for banning landmines has been modest. The result of several years of negotiations is the Convention on Certain Conventional Weapons, sometimes also known as Convention on Non-Conventional Weapons of 1980, which sought to regulate the use of landmines.

The United Nations Convention on Certain Conventional Weapons was agreed in Geneva on 10 October 1980 and entered into force in December 1982. Its aim is to ban or limit the use of certain conventional weapons considered to be excessively damaging or the effects of which are indiscriminate. The Convention established, for commanders in the field, when it was possible to use the weapon and when not, but allowed them to decide whether to apply the law in the course of the battle.

Jody Williams graduated in International Relations from the Johns Hopkins School of Advanced International Studies. She promoted the International Campaign to Ban Landmines (ICBL), which developed thanks to the work of six non-governmental organizations (Handicap International, Human Rights Watch, Medico Internacional, Mines Advisory Group, Physicians for Human Rights and the Vietnam Veterans of America Foundation), which in October 1992 met to discuss the subject of a "Joint Appeal to Ban Landmines". These organizations, united in the Head Committee of the International Campaign to Ban Landmines, called for the abolition of the use, the production, the trade and storage of landmines". The call also pushed governments to increase the resources to be devoted to demining and help to the victims.

"ICBL stands of course for International Campaign to Ban Landmines. We started out as an NGO, a non-governmental organization, with only one staff member, that is myself, helping other bigger organizations that then decided to join us. ICBL then became bigger and expanded to work in many more countries."[85]

---

85   *Ibid.*

Williams accompanied the growth of the ICBL, which currently unites over 1000 NGOs in over sixty countries, as the organizer and spokeswoman of the campaign. Working with governments, UN agencies and the International Red Cross Committee in an unprecedented cooperative initiative, the ICBL reached its aim to stipulate a first draft of an international treaty to ban landmines during the diplomatic conference held in Oslo in September 1997, to which 98 countries participated.

In Ottawa, Canada, 121 countries signed the Treaty. As a declaration of the political will for the treaty to enter into force as soon as possible, three countries ratified it at the moment of signing: Canada, Mauritius and Ireland.

For the first time, small—and medium-sized powers met to closely collaborate with the non-governmental organizations of the International Campaign to Ban Landmines and to negotiate a treaty to remove, from arsenals throughout the world, a weapon still widely used.

The strategy was to convince governments around the world to adopt national, regional and international measures to ban mines.

Thanks to her role as coordinator of the ICBL, Jody Williams wrote and spoke a great deal on the problem of landmines and the campaign for their prohibition, attending several conferences at the United Nations, the European Parliament and the Organization of the African Union. Recognizing her expertise on the subject, Williams was invited to work as a technical consultant for the UN study on the impact of armed conflict on the children of Graça Machel, the widow of Mozambique's Prime Minister.

Williams jointly wrote her first study based on two years of field research in four countries contaminated by land mines. She has authored articles for several periodicals, among which those connected to the United Nations and the Red Cross. In December 1997, the Nobel Peace Prize was awarded to the International Campaign to Ban Landmines and to its spokeswoman: Jody Williams.

One of the most important results achieved by the International Campaign is that of being able to pressure a great number of countries to sign an anti-mine treaty. These efforts have been rewarded with success: in late 1997, during the Ottawa Conference, an agreement was reached for the total ban of these weapons. Several countries have become members of the Treaty, including Italy. The treaty is called "Convention for the ban on the use, stocking, production and transferring of landmines, and for their destruction". It binds member states to refrain from using landmines, if not for training purposes related to their localization, to purifying the land or to destroy them, within four years of the Convention's entry into force in the member state in question[86]; it also obliges to refrain from developing, producing, purchasing, accumulating or transferring landmines.

Further efficacy and practicality are given to the Treaty through several provisions on financial cooperation, collaboration and technical-informational exchange between the member states and the UN and other development agencies, on demining activities and humanitarian aid. Measures of transparency and consultation among states have been introduced, to check the Treaty's operationality and on the need for revisions. The power to undertake inspections and controls on the observance of the Treaty's norms make it a remarkably complete and modern legal document.

Once ratified by the fortieth state in September 1998, the Convention formally entered into force in March 1999. Among the countries that have not signed the Ottawa Convention for the prohibition and destruction of land mines are Cuba, United States, Russia, Turkey, Egypt, Israel, Morocco, Eritrea, Somalia, Nigeria, China and India.

The Treaty approved in 1997 in Ottawa has been endorsed by 138 of the world's countries and ratified by 101 of these. The countries that produce landmines have fallen from 54 to 16, and 168 million square kilometers have been demined. The total number of removed landmines is very difficult to ascertain, although United Nations estimates, approximate as they may be, suggest the magnitude of the

---

[86] If the state declares that it is unable to ensure the destruction of all landmines in its territory, it can lodge a reasoned request for postponement of the deadline, by a maximum of ten years. The request can be renewed with adequate supporting documentation highlighting the difficulties it is encountering. This measure might seem a severe limitation of the protocol's efficacy, as it can entail a significant dilation of its most important obligations, but originates from the fact that demining is an extremely lengthy process.

problem: to date, about 100 million landmines have been buried in 62 countries.

In 1999, about 22 million landmines were destroyed, in 50 countries, but only 17 of these have entirely eliminated their landmine reserve. Of the 138 signatories, only 48 countries have published a report on the state of implementation of the Convention, although such publication is a duty for all.

Sub-Saharan Africa is the region with the highest number of active landmines still buried, especially in Angola, Burundi, Sudan, Ethiopia, DRC Congo, Rwanda, Uganda and Zimbabwe. But Afghanistan, Cambodia and Myanmar are the countries reporting the highest number of victims.

Over the last 10-20 years, the problem has taken on particularly dramatic dimensions due to the great number of civil wars and ethnic conflicts in which landmines were buried indiscriminately and in violation of the armed forces' traditional rules for their use (which require, for example, the drafting and maintenance of maps of the fields where mines are buried, to facilitate demining). Examples in point are Angola, Mozambique, Cambodia, Afghanistan, and ex-Yugoslavia.

The production of landmines is estimated at 5-10 million every year. Instead, the landmines destroyed every year in demining operations are around 100,000 and 200,000 each year. Hundreds of years would thus be necessary for the weapons to be fully removed.

Another issue worth noting is that while demining techniques for military purposes can be considered effective and readily available, those for humanitarian use are much less so.

Military demining, the purpose of which is only to open usable paths through landmines, is not at all adequate according to the standards required by humanitarian operations. The latter require the land to be 100% cleared, as the greatest humanitarian problem is precisely the return of vast spaces of land to economic activity and economic, commercial and social viability in general.

The impact of landmines on local populations' lives is devastating, since their presence closes off large portions of land from agricultural and transport use, with serious economic and psychological effects. Furthermore, all this has enormous impact on the health and social systems of the affected countries, the economic conditions of which are usually dramatic. It is estimated that the cost of artificial limbs for those maimed by landmines is about $3,000. Considering the large number of these invalids (for example, in Cambodia, where it is believed that between 4 and 7 million landmines are still buried, and where one out of every 236 people has been mutilated by a landmine), the dimensions of the problem are clear.

Moreover, technological advances have greatly exacerbated the situation: the current generation of landmines is made with plastic materials, which makes them extremely hard to detect. Also, mines with highly sophisticated mechanisms have been developed, which make them dangerous to even search and remove, thus posing serious risks even for professionals engaged in demining.

There are currently two methods used for minesweeping. The first entails the use of dogs or pigs trained to recognize unexploded mines by smell; the second, which can be used only for metallic mines, exploits the changes in magnetic field generated by the presence of metallic masses within the range of the sensor. Other techniques are currently being studied.

Today, Jody Williams teaches courses for international social workers at the Graduate College of Social Work, University of Houston.

CHAPTER 14

VANDANA SHIVA

(Dehra Dunh, 5 November 1952-)

The law on seeds and a patented world

Vandana Shiva was born in 1952, in a city in Uttar Pradesh, in northeastern India.

Her father was a forest guard, while her mother was a schoolteacher who had become a farmer after the bloody India-Pakistan war in 1947-48. Her parents' home frequently hosted intellectuals and disciples of Mahatma Gandhi. Vandana spent her childhood close to the earth: first, the farm managed by her mother, and then among the Rajasthan forests, close to the Indian scientific universities from which she graduated in physics.

In Canada, she obtained her Ph.D. from the University of Western Ontario. She then decided to give up a career in the United States to return to India, to contribute to society and understand her country better.

She visits the places of her childhood, among the Himalaya mountains, and no longer sees as many forests and rivers as she used to; in their place were now dams and highways. To make space for great apple orchards, entire forests of oaks had been felled, even though these played a crucial role in absorbing the violent monsoon rains and prevent floods. She also noticed that the quality of life had changed: the population was forced to live in slums, which consequently impoverished their economic and social status. The trip led her to join the Chipko movement (named after a legendary poet), which united women who fought against the destruction of forests, the forests from which they derived their sustenance.

In 1981, the authorities were forced to recognize the wisdom of Chipko's philosophy, according to which the truly valuable parts of forests are their soil, water and pure air. Felling timber was banned beyond 1000 meters of altitude. "It was the Chipko movement to awaken my conscience and show me that there is a connection between the destruction of the environment and the increase in poverty"[87]. "Commercial cultivation does not take into account the forest's general value: it measures the value only in terms of the quantity of wood that the industry yields. For example, stubble is useful for nourishing the soil, for fertilizing the earth where animals graze, and that villagers use to build their dwellings. Yet it began to be treated as waste. This blindness towards the needs of nature and man has destroyed the possibility of satisfying them and has impoverished the soil. Therefore, populations do not have sufficient and adequate food, and were forced to contract debt to buy the necessary food. Instead of developing and enhancing the value of the 8,500 species used for human consumption, the agricultural sector has reduced crops to only eight products sold on global markets."[88]

Vandana began to fight for seed freedom. What does this mean?

Industry representatives openly declared their aims: they wanted to genetically modify crops so that they could be defined "new organisms" and be patented as intellectual property, as one would do with inventions. This would give rise to a property right over seeds. Indeed, multinational corporations needed an international treaty to allow them to patent seeds: this was how the issue of patents on forms of life was included in World Trade Organization agreements.

The seed dictatorship was established through patents which make seeds an intellectual property of multinational corporations, and prohibit farmers from using them freely; through laws on seeds that introduce licensing and registration requirements, and make seed crossing and exchange illegal; and through technologies that genetically modify seeds to make the second generation of seeds sterile and thus force farmers to buy new ones[89].

---

[87] Vandana Shiva, *Storia dei Semi*, Feltrinelli, Milan, 2012, p. 8.

[88] *Ibid.*, p. 12.

[89] *Ibid.*, pp.15-16.

"Our duty, that is to preserve all the seeds of the world, has become a crime. This was what led Vandana Shiva to found Navdanya ("nine seeds", but also "new gift").

Vandana Shiva says she thought of the name while watching a farmer who had planted nine different types of seeds on a single plot of land. It is a movement which aims to safeguard plant species and the preservation and sharing of seeds among farmers. Navdanya has created over 100 "seed banks", thanks to which the 65,000 members can freely keep and exchange seeds.

Today, Navdanya has over 70,000 members, mostly women, who practice organic farming in 16 States of India, a network of 65 "seed banks" that keep about 6,000 authoctonous species, and the Bija Vidyapeeth, or Seed School, which teaches "sustainable living".

"Our plants have proved to be better able at nourishing us than those traded on a large scale around the world, and less demanding. The rice crops that resort to chemicals need 2500 millimeters of rain every year, while our plants are satisfied with 200-300 millimeters.

The supporters of industrial farming, based on a single crop, argue that this produces more food and greater wealth. We are certain that our system, called *baranaja*, and that envisages the use of twelve different seeds (from buckwheat to wild soya) produce double the amount of food and triple the amount of wealth that we would receive from maize alone.

Highly diversified farming is more effective than extensive farming."[90]

"in 1981, the Ministry for the Environment asked me to study the disastrous effect of mining activities in the Doon Valley. The mining had destroyed the ecosystem.

My report was drafted on the basis of a research performed in collaboration with other scholars, and gave rise to a strong popular movement that led to a case before the Supreme Court, which finally prohibited mining in that Valley in 1983. On 12 March 1985, the Supreme Court was called upon to judge a public interest case against limestone mining in the Doon Valley, and ordered the permanent or temporary closure of 53 upon 60 quarries within the geographical confines of the Doon Valley or the Dehradun Tehsil. The highest court gave the following reasoning:

---

[90]   *Ibid.*, p. 17.

This is the first case in the country on issues related to the environment and ecological balance. The issues to be considered are of great importance not only for those who live within the Mussoorie chain, part of the Himalayas, but also for their implications for the well-being of the general population of the country. It clearly focuses on the conflict between development and conservation and contributes to highlight the need to reconcile the two, in the country's broader interest.

The Court justified halting the mining activities as:

. . . the price to pay for protecting and safeguarding the people's right to live in a healthy environment with minimal disruption of the ecological equilibrium, and without avoidable risks to it and its livestock, homes and cultivated land, and without unduly affecting the air, water and environment.

With this judgment, the Supreme Court of India established a precedent, stating that a stable and healthy environment is a human right, and intervened in favor of the people for fair and sustainable development[91].

In 1999, a terrible cyclone hit Orissa, a State of eastern India: the storm killed 30,000 people. Vandana Shiva created seed banks—called "seeds of hope"—that can help farmers to face environmental disasters. The banks collect, keep, multiply and distribute seeds where necessary; these seeds are capable of resisting droughts, floods and cyclones. The farmers are very good at selecting and crossing breeds resistant to salt and insufficient or excess water.

The food industry, with its scientific methods of selection, is not able to face climate changes and the alternation of floods and droughts that these entail.

In 2002, along with one of her fellow militants—Satish Kumar, an ex-monk—in the Doon Valley in northern India, Vandana founded a rather special Seed School, where sustainable life, solidarity and peace are studied.

"A seed collects within it millions of years of natural evolution, but also all the changes that farmers have achieved in the course of millennia, thanks to their selection. And we know that these seeds

---

[91]   Vandana Shiva, *Dalla parte degli ultimi. Una via per i diritti dei contadini*, Slow Food, 2008, p. 54.

possess the capacity to continue evolving, generating plants with ever more different traits, for millions of years yet. In a seed, there is both past and present.

Seeds do not live alone. They preserve the memory of their place of birth and of the relations they had with other forms of life, such as bees and butterflies: the flowers born from these seeds gave their pollen to bees and butterflies, which carried it to fertilize other plants and enable other seeds to be born. Plants reproduce by means of their flowers: from flowers come seeds, from which, season after season, year after year, new plants grow.

But the relations between the seed and its surroundings do not end here: in the soil, millions of minuscule organisms live. These nourish the seed and the plant and enable the plant to grow more or less strong; in turn, these tiny organisms are nourished by the substances produced by the seed and by the plant."[92]

Hybrid seeds are obtained from two plants of the same species, but different breeds. In this case, the pollination mechanism is the same, but human intervention is necessary. Hybrid plants force farmers to buy seeds each season because these seeds cannot simply be collected and kept, as is done with native seeds.

Seeds born from natural pollination are self-reproducing: they are a renewable resource that is never exhausted. After harvest, the farmers save them to be used the next season.

Hybrid seeds and genetically modified seeds are non-renewable products that must be bought again every year.

The Navdanya farms in India have shown that in farms where there are several different forms of life, food can be produced in large amounts without any need for external aids or chemicals. Thanks to certain plants and animals, the soil becomes fertile again, and we can keep parasites and weeds away. The soil gives what is necessary to nourish worms and other useful organisms, and to raise the farm animals, thus obtaining food for those who work the land and raise the livestock, and, finally, even products for sale.

The farming industry produced seeds created to grow into plants with sterile seeds, and others which revive only if they come into contact with certain substances (which, naturally, farmers are forced to buy).

---

[92]   Shiva, at note 1, pp. 31-33.

The loss of local species and variety brings to the irreversible loss of the genetic diversity they contain, among which the genes for adapting to the conditions in which they evolved. This genetic erosion has dangerously reduced the genetic pool available for natural and farmer/human selection. As a consequence, agricultural crops are more vulnerable to sudden climate changes and new parasites and diseases.

For example, in the United States, in the 1970s the fungus *Helminthosporium maydis* destroyed over half of the corn crops in the southern part of the country.

GMO crops have not managed to defeat neither parasites nor weeds. Actually, the reverse has happened: GMO seeds have led to the evolution of super-resistant parasites.

In Canada, Monsanto markets its Bt potato as a highly eco-friendly product, as it releases a biodegradable and natural pesticide that kills only the insects that attack that particular field. In reality, the situation is very different; the Bt plant never stops producing its toxins, and continued contact with these toxins, some parasites, such as a certain type of cotton-eating moth, become resistant to that poison and thus much more harmful. The toxin is also capable of seriously damaging "good" insects like ladybirds and bees.

In China, where transgenic cotton is very popular, some bugs which previously posed no problem, suddenly became a cause for huge concern: from 1997 to today, their population has grown by twelve times.

Neem is a beautiful tropical tree which originated in India. Among its qualities are that of keeping pests away. Indeed, its leaves contain a natural "arsenal", which keeps away harmful insects, worms, fungi and bacteria. The presence of this tree enables the cultivation of healthy crops, without resorting to pesticides and insecticides.

In 1994, the anti-parasite and antifungal properties of neem were patented as "inventions". The United States government and the American multinational corporation W.R. Grace were granted the patent on an oil extracted form neem seeds: as if the plants' antifungal properties had not been discovered years before by farmers. W.R. Grace bought all the neem seeds available to make its anti-parasite oil, such that farmers could no longer find any seeds. Vandana thus launched another campaign to collect signatures. In March 2005, after ten more years, the European Patent Office revoked the patent previously granted to the American Ministry of Agriculture and W.R. Grace.

In another case, on July 8, 1994, RiceTec Inc., a Texas company, lodged an application with the United States Patents and Trademarks Office to patent basmati rice. The Texan company claimed to have invented a new breed of the plant. On the basis of that patent, it would have been necessary to seek RiceTec Inc.'s consent before sowing and harvesting. On this occasion too, Vandana organized protests and demonstrations, and pressured the Indian government to oppose the application. In the end, the Patents and Trademarks Office denied RiceTec Inc.'s application for basmati rice, and allowed it only for certain hybrid breeds of rice[93].

For her enormous effort in favor of the Indian population and the environment, in 1993 Vandana Shiva was awarded the Alternative Nobel Peace Prize, also known as "Right Livelihood Award".

In 1998, in Bratislava, Slovakia, Vandana established "Diverse Women for Diversity", a movement of women involved in food, agriculture, patents and biotechnology.

In 2004, with the British Schumacher College, she founded Bija Vidyapeeth, an international university for sustainability.

"Our law of the seed seeds to change the current paradigm" she explained. "There is European legislation that prevents farmers from using their own seeds and therefore violates seed sovereignty. The only way to protect farmers and jobs, diversity and food, is to fight for seed sovereignty."

"As long as humanity considered the Earth as a mother, rivers flowed clean, forests were lush, the soil conserved its fertility, while biodiversity flourished and climate patterns were stable and predictable. [. . .] Instead, the destruction of nature and of the cultures

---

[93] *Ibid.*, p.

forged by Mother Earth coincide with diseases of the environment and of those who inhabit it."[94]

The Law of the Seed

Part 1—Conservation of agricultural biodiversity

Article 1—Overall objective of diversity
Legislation shall not run against the overall objective of conservation and enrichment of diversity.

Article 3—Plant genetic resources as commons
Plant genetic resources for food and agriculture shall be considered as commons.

Article 11—Research programs
Public research programs shall give priority, *inter alia*, to:

- Understanding farmers' knowledge of breeding;
- Broaden the genetic base of crops and increase the range of genetic diversity available;
- Promote the use of local and locally adapted crops, varieties and underutilized species;

---

[94] Shiva, at note 5, p. 19.

Other books consulted: Vandana Shiva, *Fare pace con la terra*, Feltrinelli, Milan, 2012 (Italian translation of *Making Peace with the Earth*, New Delhi, Women Unlimited, 2012); Vandana Shiva, *Il bene comune della terra*, Feltrinelli, Milan, 2011 (Italian translation of *Earth Democracy: Justice, Sustainability and Peace*, South End Press, 2005); Vandana Shiva, *India spezzata. Diversità e democrazia sotto attacco*, Il saggiatore, Milan, 2011 (Italian translation of *India Divided: Diversity and Democracy Under Attack*, Seven Stories Press, 2003); Vandana Shiva, *Campi di battaglia. Biodiversità e agricoltura industriale*, Edizione Ambiente, 2009; Vandana Shiva, *Semi del suicidio*, Odradek, Rome, 2009 (Italian translation of *Seeds of Suicide: The Ecological and Human Costs of Globalization of Agriculture*, Zed Books Ltd, 2005); Vandana Shiva, *Ritorno alla terra. La fine dell'ecoimperialismo*, Fazi, Rome, 2009; Vandana Shiva, *Il mondo sotto brevetto*, Feltrinelli, Milan, 2002.

- Strengthen the capacity to develop varieties particularly adapted to concrete social, economic and ecological conditions, including marginal areas;
- Enhance and conserve plant genetic resources by maximizing intra—and inter-specific variation for the benefit of farmers, especially those who generate and use their own varieties and apply ecological principles to maintain soil fertility and to combat diseases, weeds and pests;
- Gather knowledge and information of underutilised crops and wild relatives of food crops.

Part 3—Farmers' Rights

Article 13—Farmers' rights

Farmers' rights to freely breed and produce, save and exchange, share or sell shall be fully recognised in accordance with the freedom of trade and commerce under national and international law, in particular with

- the Protection of Plant Varieties and Farmers' Rights Act 2001 of India, and
- article 9 on Farmers' Rights of the International Treaty on Plant Genetic Resources for Food and Agriculture, and shall be interpreted in this context and shall be fully respected and implemented both at national and international levels.

Recognition of the contribution of local communities and indigenous and farmers' rights, referred to in Article 9 of the international treaty, can also be achieved through systems of collective ownership of local varieties implemented by the public at the regional level and/or local level.

Article 14—Right to Exchange

The gift or exchange of seed of any variety, or its placing on the market, shall be governed by the principles of seed sovereignty.

Farmers, seed savers and gardeners cannot be prosecuted or criminalized for any activity related to exchange of seeds and plant reproductive material belonging to the public domain.

CHAPTER 15

REGGIE LITTLEJOHN

Defending conceived children: a gift from God

The story of the lawyer Reggie Littlejohn does not begin in the field of human rights.

She graduated from Yale Law School and became a lawyer. For about eight years, she worked in tax and commercial law, in San Francisco.

"During that time, I represented some Chinese refugees in their application for asylum in the United States".

Littlejohn later successfully followed other two cases of women who had been victims of the one-child policy.

The Population and Family Planning Law, enacted in 2001 by the People's Republic of China, sought to achieve the economic and social well-being of the collectivity and the improvement of the Chinese families' happiness (Article 1).

"Then I fell seriously sick, and began to pray for all the people who were worse off than me. When I recovered, I began to write a screenplay that later became the movie "Pearls of China", in which I tell the tragic story of these women. I then founded Women's Rights Without Frontiers'."

Many people know that in China, there is a law establishing a one-child policy; however, what many may not be aware of is that in order to enforce it, the Government forces women to abort and to undergo sterilization[95].

On 22 April 2009, the Secretary of State Hillary Clinton condemned forced abortion and forced sterilization in China. During a

---

[95]   Article in the publication *A sua immagine*, n. 41, 19 october 2013, p. 31.

Congressional Hearing before the House Foreign Affairs Committee, she stated that these practices are "absolutely unacceptable" and "an egregious interference with women's rights."[96]

The law on the only child was ordered by Deng Xiaoping in the late 1970s, and is the basis of China's family planning policy.

"There are no logical reasons to keep in force the law on the only child. First, this policy has reduced the workforce and the country is already losing much business to other countries which have a greater and cheaper workforce. Second, because of what I call the 'China senior tsunami'.

The law had deep effects on the birth rate: after the population boom of Mao's era, where women had on average 5.9 children each, today the rate has fallen to 1.7. But those born during that boom are now aging and retiring, and there are not enough youths to take care of them, nor a social security program. It seems that we are watching a slow-motion demographic disaster. Finally, there is a problem of imbalance between the genders. Today, in China, there are 37 million more men than women, and this destabilizes society[97]. [. . .]

Littlejohn launched a suggestively-named campaign: "Save a girl". In China, she explains, "we have an underground network of activists who work on the field and are able to identify women who have undergone sex determination tests who do not wish to have a daughter, who are about to abort or who have had a daughter and have decided to abandon her. When we find them, we tell them not to abort and not to abandon these creatures only because they are female. We offer them a monthly stipend for one year, with which to raise the child. In 90% of cases, the women decided to keep their daughters".

Women's Rights Without Frontiers also supports women who flee from forced abortions.

Reggie is prominently featured in "It's a Girl," the authoritative documentary film about gendercide in China and India. She premiered the film at the European and British Parliaments in November 2012 and in Capitol Hill Visitors Center Auditorium in Washington, DC in April, 2013. She screened the film three times at the United Nations Conference on the Status of Women in March, 2013.

---

[96]   http://www.womensrightswithoutfrontiers.org/index.php?nav=hillary_clinton.
[97]   Article at note 1, p. 31.

Reggie has appeared thirteen times on Voice of America, the official U.S. broadcast into China, Taiwan and Hong Kong. WRWF has the only Chinese website in the world dedicated to exposing the brutal truth about forced abortion in China.

An acclaimed international expert on China's One Child Policy, Reggie has testified six times at the United States Congress, three times at the European Parliament, and she has presented at the British, Irish and Canadian Parliaments as well.

During the 10th International Conference on Maternal Health held in Rome, 2013, Littlejohn affirmed that "every life is a gift of God. And fighting to save it is a duty of every Christian".

CHAPTER 16

MICHELLE ROBINSON OBAMA

(Chicago, 17 January 1964-)

"Vote for Michelle's husband"

"Fraser Robinson worked the swing shift in the boiler room at the city's water purification plant, while Marian stayed home to take care of Michelle and her brother, Craig, sixteen months Michelle's senior. Michelle's father went off to work uncomplainingly each day, even after he was diagnosed with multiple sclerosis at the age of thirty."[98]

The Chicago where Michelle was born tended to privilege whites, and was a place where black workers still had little chance to develop a career. Things slowly began to change when she was still a child. Thanks to the civil rights movements of the 1960s, the Civil Rights Act of 1960 and the Voting Rights Act of 1964 were enacted, and African-American leaders such as Rev. Martin Luther King and Malcolm X became symbols for a new generation of black people.

During Michelle's childhood, the South Side was a predominantly black metropolitan neighborhood: here, the Robinsons taught their children to work hard, to aim high and to never give up.

Craig Robinson, currently the coach of the University of Oregon's basketball team, declared to the Washington Post "When you grow up as a black kid in a white world, so many times people are telling

---

[98] Elisabeth Lightfoot, *Michelle Obama. First Lady della Speranza*, Nutrimenti, Rome, 2009, p. 27.

you, sometimes not maliciously, sometimes maliciously, you're not good enough [. . .] To have a family, which we did, who constantly reminded you how smart you were, how good you were, how pleasant it was to be around you, how successful you could be, it's hard to combat. Our parents gave us a little head start by making us feel confident."[99]

After graduating from Princeton and Harvard Law School, Michelle accepted a job offer from the prestigious law firm Sidley & Austin. She specialized in marketing and intellectual property cases, also dealing with transactions and antitrust. She also worked with other lawyers on representing AT&T, the communications giant, when it made an initial public offer for NCR Corporation[100].

In working on an agreement with ARCO, Michelle impressed the lawyer representing Union Carbide. Nate Eimer, an ex-lawyer at Sidley Austin, told the National Law Journal that Michelle "stood out from the average associate lawyer. She waited to be sure of what she wanted to say before speaking. Her analysis was clear and precise".

After one year in that law firm, Michelle was charged with following an especially promising summer intern. For Sidley, Michelle and the intern, that meeting turned out to be pivotal. The intern was Barack Obama, who would later become Michelle's boyfriend and husband. His beliefs and work for the community and society would finally draw Michelle from her promising career in the private sector to start an equally successful one in the public sector.

Michelle Obama explained that her work at Sidley & Austin allowed her to pay off part of her student loan, but did not fulfill her wish to work for a better world. In summer 1989, with Barack (who was not yet her boyfriend), she went to Altgeld Gardens, a poor part of the South Side, where he had worked as local coordinator before enrolling in law school.

Michelle was enchanted by Barack's speech, which he delivered to an audience consisting primarily of poor African-American women. He spoke of the chance to fight to change one's own situation

---

[99] Peter Slevin, "Her Heart's in the Race", *Washington Post*, 28 November 2007.

[100] Dan Slater, "Campaign '08: Michelle Obama's Sidley Austin Years", on the "law" blog of the *wall Street Journal*, 23 June 2008, http://blogs.wsj.com/law/2008/06/23/campaign-08-michelle-obamas-sidleyaustin-years.

even when everything seems wrong and everything is against you. He exhorted them to imagine a "world as it could be", instead of accepting "the world as it is".

Michelle was about twenty-five years old and was rapidly soaring in the law firm, perhaps spurred by those "conservative values" that led her to "aim for the same goals as my white classmates", as she had written in her Princeton graduation thesis.

The summer that Michelle met Barack, she was beginning to think of why, perhaps, she no longer wanted to be part of that world.

Some months after meeting her future husband, other two events changed her life. Her beloved father, Fraser, passed away unexpectedly after an operation, and Michelle also lost a dear friend, Suzanne Alele, who died of cancer at only twenty-five. She had been Michelle's roommate in Princeton and one of Michelle's closest friends. That double loss brought Michelle to review her life: "I was confronted for the first time in my life with the fact that nothing was really guaranteed", she stated in a public speech before a Party assembly in Iowa. "One of the things I remembered about Suzanne is that she always made decisions that would make her happy and create a level of fulfillment. She was less concerned with pleasing other people, and thank God. Was I waking up every morning feeling excited about work and the work I was doing? I needed to figure out what I really loved"[101].

In the interview for The Telegraph, Michelle described her journey towards the decision that she later took. She first posed questions to herself and then to others. The loss of her father and of her friend "showed her that she could die the next day", she explained to the journalist. "I had to ask myself: 'is this how I want to spend my time?' I knew I would never feel a sense of passion or joy about the law. I was on a conveyor belt. Law school had just been the next step."

In 1991, her questioning led her to a crisis, and she met some friends to discuss the possibility of passing to the public sector. One of them put her in touch with Valerie Jarrett, general secretary of Mayor Daley, and who from that moment became a friend and constant guide for Michelle.

When Michelle met Mrs. Jarrett in her town hall office, she explained her situation: she had a great job in a prestigious law firm,

---

[101] Slevin, *cit.*

she had a good salary, but she was not happy. When she told people that she was starting to think of leaving her job for a less-paid job in public service, most people thought she was crazy.

Jarrett did not; after graduating from Stanford and Michigan Law School, she had reached a similar decision some years later.

"We understood each other immediately", said Michelle in an interview for the Chicago Tribune. "Valerie knew how I felt. It was hard to find people who could understand my decision to leave such a high-paying job. But she had had my same feelings, the wish to do more for the community, for a life that was civically satisfying[102].

Recognizing a kindred spirit, other than a highly-qualified candidate, Jarrett immediately offered her a job. Michelle signed her contract. Valerie Jarrett would later help Michelle to gain a series of posts in public service and would suggest to her husband to run for President of the United States.

When Michelle announced her wish to leave Sidley & Austin, everyone was sad.

Although the new job provided her with a much lower salary, Michelle believed that that type of work would have brought her greater satisfaction. She was prepared for changing things in the public service. "What she had learned at Harvard Law School and Sidley & Austin has served her well in all of the judgments she has had to make as an administrator and manager".

For Michelle, working in the Mayor's office was only the first of several posts in the public and, later, non-profit sectors. According to Valerie, Michelle Obama is a priceless resource in any occupational situation, especially when it comes to managing group dynamics. Of course, Michelle was diligent and competent, but her added value was her willingness to deal with issues directly.

In 1993, Michelle accepted another position close to her heart: she assumed the leadership of the Chicago section of Public Allies, a program that leads youth to apprenticeships in the world of public service, with internships in non-profit organizations. The program had been developed within Bill Clinton's AmeriCorps project. Working in that environment meant, for Michelle, working to shape a "world as it should be", instead of remaining within the confines of

---

[102] Don Terry, "In the Path of Lightning", *Chicago tribune*, 27 July 2008.

"the world as it is". The role was especially suited to Michelle, since she was "really good at taking nothing and pulling something out", said Valerie Jarrett.

Before leaving Public Allies for the University of Chicago, Michelle reunited an influential management board and raised so much money that when she left, in 1996, her office had "stock for about a year, which had never happened before in any of our offices" said Paul Schmitz, CEO of Public Allies: "she had built something lasting".

Michelle's new job at the University of Chicago was based on the same ideals that had led her to Public Allies. As Vice-President of the Student Services Center and Director of the University's Community Service Center, Michelle intervened in the coordination of student volunteer work and could help other youths who were devising their own "motivational hierarchies". In that period, Michelle also became a mother: first Malia, born in 1998, and Sasha, born in 2001.

In the meantime, Barack Obama had started his political career, and between electoral campaigns and commitments, Michelle was often deprived of her spouse's support, especially in caring for their daughters. These dynamics gave her an entirely different perspective of what it meant to be a working woman.

After some years at the University (and one year after being a mother of two young girls), Michelle's reputation came to the attention of the President of the Chicago Hospital Consortium, Michael Riordan. In 2002, Riordan summoned Michelle for an interview. Michelle was hired as executive director of the Chicago University Hospital Community Affairs, a role that required her to maintain links between the hospital and its neighborhood. Among its various goals, the hospital hoped to open some clinics in the South Side, where Michelle had grown up.

In 2005, Michelle was promoted to Vice-President for External Affairs.

Riordan was not the only one to praise Michelle. "In community affairs, you're dealing with a range of people, from presidents of hospitals to community leaders to people who are poor . . . and she just has a way about her, a real kindness," said Susan Sher, the hospital's legal counsel.

In the press release announcing Michelle's promotion, Riordan said: "We have been impressed with the care, imagination and energy that Michelle has brought to every project she has worked on since coming to the Hospitals. We are excited to have her join the ranks of senior management. She has brings to our team a new level of compassion, commitment, and close connections to the community"[103].

As for Michelle's private life, she told the Chicago Sun-Times: "Barack and I have interesting lives, never did." "We're basically family people. When we go on a date, it's either dinner or a movie because we can't stay awake for both"[104]. An element that has surely contributed to the good development of their union is their wish to act as role models for their children, and to support each other in this. On her Facebook page, under "Activities", Michelle Obama lists "Hanging out with my husband Barack and our daughters. Hitting the campaign trail. Working out." Under "Interests", we find: "Being a mom, Sudoku". Under "Favorite movie": "I've only gotten to see kids' movies recently—saw Enchanted not too long ago." In "Favorite Books:" "We read a lot of kids' books at our house".

Another "secret" of their marriage is their faith, their mutual trust, and their faith in the future. Although she was initially reluctant to give her blessing to Barack's presidential campaign, Michelle said that, from the moment when she thought of what his candidacy would have meant for her daughters and for their future, she could no longer stop.

When Barack introduces Michelle, he calls her "his rock", because, as he says, she keeps him grounded.

Once, in an interview, Michelle said "Barack didn't pledge riches, only a life that would be interesting. On that promise he's delivered"[105].

Every time she is asked for her plans as a First Lady, Michelle answers that her first priority is raising her daughters Malia and Sasha. Or, as she said in February 2008, "To make sure my kids have

---

[103] University of Chicago Hospitals, "Michelle Obama Appointed Vice President to Community and External Affairs at the University of Chicago Hospitals", 9 May 2005, www.uchospitals.edu/news/2005/20050509-obama.html.

[104] Jill Lawrence, "Michelle's Homemaker Side", Chicago SunTimes, 1 July 2008.

[105] Sheri Stritof, Bob Stritof, "Barack and Michelle Obama Marriage Profile", http://marriage.about.com/od/celebritymarriage/p/barackobama.

their heads on straight. We can talk about the high-falutin' notion of a First Spouse platform, but here I am, a woman professional who has to work on top of my first job as a mother"[106].

According to Earnest Harris, it is fair to watch a potential president's wife closely, especially if the spouse actively participates in the campaign, because "she is a good barometer of the candidate's judgment", and because one day she might represent the country "at least in an unofficial way". But "why does Michelle spark such a high level of rancor from those on the far right?" he asked. Nicknames such as "baby mama" and "angry black woman" exceed by far "the limits of decent and fair political discourse, even in its present state"[107]. Why all this resentment? According to Harris, the answer is related to the issue of race: "I suspect that part of the focus on Michelle Obama is the fact that she has a double negative in the eyes of some. She is an intelligent, strong African-American woman, and I suspect for some this is really hard to handle".

At the speech before the Democratic national convention, she spoke of her parents and her brother, and of how she and her husband were the embodiment of the American Dream. She spoke of the men and women who had paved the way so that her husband could run for the White House, and of the "thread that connects our hearts". There was no bitterness in her words.

"Towards the end of her speech, she spoke about herself and Barack as parents and the way their hopes and dreams for their own daughters mirror the hopes and dreams all parents have for their children. [. . .]" Of how they listened to their hopes and not their fears. Of how they "decided to stop doubting and start dreaming: "in this great country—where a girl from the South Side of Chicago can go to college and law school, and the son of a single mother from Hawaii can go all the way to the White House—we committed ourselves to building the world as it should be".

---

[106] Monica Langley, "Michelle Obama Solidifies Her Role in the Election", *Wall Street Journal*, 11 February 2008.

[107] Earnest Harris, "Cal Thomas's Scary Angy Black Michelle", *Huffington Post*, from the "Off the Bus" blog, 2 July 2008, www.huffington-post.com/earnest-harris/cal-thomass-scary-angry-b_b_110588-html.

On 4 November 2008, hope triumphed. Barack Obama became the 44th President of the United States of America.

Martin Luther King's memorial day fell on the 19th of that month. The Obamas devoted the whole day to services of social interest. As Michelle had written in a newsletter dated 12 January 2009 to her supporters: "Barack and I will volunteer in Washington, our new home. We hope you will join us in serving your communities. To put this country back on its feet, all citizens must work together for a common goal."

THANKS

I thank all staff of the Italian Book Club www.theitalianbookclub.com for support in promoting my book.

BIBLIOGRAPHY
AND WEBSITES

DEBORA
Elena Bosetti, *Donne della Bibbia*. Cittadella editrice, Assisi 2009.

ANTIGONE
G. Perrotta. *Disegno storico della letteratura greca*. Principato Editore, Milan 1964.
G. Tarditi. *Storia della letteratura greca*. Loescher, Turin, 1973.

ELEONORA D'ARBOREA
Bianca Pitzorno, *Vita di Eleonora d'Arborea. Principessa medioevale di Sardegna*, Mondadori 2010.
Francesco Cesare Casula, *Eleonora regina del regno di Arborea*, Carlo Delfino Editore, Sassari, 2004.
Camillo Bellienu, *Eleonora d'Arborea*, Ilisso edizioni, Nuoro, 2004.
Stefania De Michele *L'arcano minore Eleonora d'Arborea tra mito e realtà*. Ethos edizioni, Oliena Nuoro, 2007.
Carta de Logu http://www.fontesarda.it/sr/cartaind.htm

BERTHA VON SUTTNER
Nicola Sinopoli *Una donna per la pace*. Fratelli Palombi editore, Rome 1986

SUFFRAGGETTE
A. Valle. A. Coviello. *Anch'io ho votato Repubblica* Edizioni Giacché, La Spezia.
Mary Wollstonecraft "Il manifesto femminista". Edizioni Elle, Milan 1977.

EGLANTYNE JEBB

Eglantyne Jebb: *"Cambridge; A brief study in social questions"* 1906. General Books, Memphis, Tennessee, 2010.

Linda Mahood: *"Feminism and voluntary action" Eglantyne Jebb and Save the Children, 1876-1928.* Palgrave Macmillian, New York 2009.

Clare Mulley: *"The woman who saved the children. A biography of Eglantyne Jebb founder of Save The Children".* Oneworld. Oxford 2009.

www.savethechildren.it

LIDIA POET—LINA FURLAN

Clara Bounous *La Toga Negata* Alzani Pinerolo, Turin, 1997.

Dino Segre *Pitigrilli parla di Pitigrilli*, Sonzogno, Milan,1949

ELEONOR ROOSEVELT

Blanche Wiesen Cook, *Eleanor Roosevelt*, New York: Viking Press, 1992.

Mary Ann Glandon *Verso un mondo nuovo*. Liberilibri, Macerata, 2001

Eleonor Roosevelt *The autobiography of Eleanor Roosevelt*. Harper & Brothers, New York 1961

Eleanor Roosevelt, *On My Own* New York: Harper, 1958

SHIRIN EBADI

Shirin Ebadi: Il mio Iran. Sperling & Kupfer 2007 Milan.

Shrin Ebadi *"La gabbia d'oro"*. Bur Rizzoli 2008 Milan.

HILLARY CLINTON

Hillary Rhodam Clinton "La mia vita. La mia storia". Sperling & Kupfer, Milan, 2003.

Hillary Rodham Clinton "It Takes a Village". Pocket books

JODY WILLIAMS

Roberts and Jody Williams *After the Guns Fall Silent: The Enduring Legacy of Landmines* di Shaw, Vietnam Veterans of America Foundation, Washington, 1995.

Jody Williams. Landmines and measures to eliminate them, International Review of the Red Cross, nr 370/luglio-agosto 1995.

Jody Williams. Landmines: Dealing with the Environmental Impact, Enviroment Security, 1997.Vol. 1. No. 2."

Jody Williams. Social Consequences of Widesread Use of Landmines, Landmine Symposium, International Committee of the Red Cross, Montreux, Svizzera, aprile 1993.

Jody Williams. The Protection if Children Against Landmines and Unexploded Ordinance, in "Impatto del conflitto armato sui bambini: rapporto del gruppo di esperti del Segretario Generale di Graca Machel, A/51/306, 26 agosto 1996.

VANDANA SHIVA

Vandana Shiva. Storia dei semi Feltrinelli, Milan, 2013.

Vandana Shiva. Fare la pace con la terra. Feltrinelli, Milan, 2012.

Vandana Shiva. Il bene comune della terra. Feltrinelli Milan, 2011.

Vandana Shiva. India spezzata. Diversità e democrazia sotto attacco. Il saggiatore, Milan, 2011.

Vandana Shiva. Campi di battaglia. Biodiversità e agricoltura industriale. Edizione ambiente, Milan, 2009.

Vandana Shiva. Semi del suicidio. Odradek, Rome, 2009.

Vandana Shiva. Ritorno alla terra. La fine dell'ecoimperialismo. Fazi, Rome, 2009.

Vandana Shiva. Dalla parte degli ultimi. Una via per i diritti dei contadini. Slow Food, Firenze, 2008.

Vandana Shiva. Le guerre dell'acqua. Feltrinelli, Milan,2004.

Vandana Shiva. Il mondo sotto brevetto. Feltrinelli, Milan, 2002.

REGGIE LITTLEJOHN
www.womensrightswithoutfrontiers.org

MICHELLE OBAMA

Elizabeth Lightfoot: *Michelle Obama. First Lady della speranza.* Nutrimenti, Rome, 2009.

Liza Mundy: *Michelle. La biografia.* Castelvecchi editore, Isola del Liri (Fr) 2009.